One of His Boys

One of His Boys

The Letters of Johnnie Pickle and His Mentor, George Washington Carver

JOHN H. PICKLE JR.

NEWSOUTH BOOKS
Montgomery

NewSouth Books
105 S. Court Street
Montgomery, AL 36104

Publisher's Cataloging-in-Publication Data
Names: Pickle, John H., Jr., author. | Pickle, Johnnie, author.
| Carver, George W., author.
Title: One of his boys / by John H. Pickle Jr.
Description: Montgomery : NewSouth [2021]
Identifiers: LCCN 2021932467 | ISBN 9781588383716
Subjects: Carver, George Washington, 1864–1943 |
Scientists—Biography. | Letters—Biography.

The photographs featured throughout this book are courtesy
of John H. Pickle Jr. The photographs included between
pages 62 and 75 are from the Polk Collection of the Tuskegee
University Archives and are used courtesy of that institution.

Printed in the United States of America

 *The Black Belt, defined by its dark, rich soil, stretches
across central Alabama. It was the heart of the cotton belt.
It was and is a place of great beauty, of extreme wealth
and grinding poverty, of pain and joy. Here we take our
stand, listening to the past, looking to the future.*

To the memory of George W. Carver, his talent, and the impact of those talents, which have been passed forward for generations. He was a man of God, a talented artist, an exceptional scientist, a leader in racial healing, and a promoter of racial harmony as an inspirational speaker.

The world is a better place because of this man and the spirit, academic skills, and personal gifting demonstrated throughout his life.

Contents

Preface

George Washington Carver was an African American scientist known as the "Wizard of Tuskegee" who served as a mentor to my father Johnnie Pickle beginning in 1932. A chance meeting between Carver and Pickle occurred in the spring of that year. Pickle had been assigned as a guide at Ole Miss for Carver as they searched for natural props to support a speech that the scientist was to give that same evening under the auspices of the YMCA. A number of letters were exchanged over the next few years. After Carver took a bad fall in 1938, his strength was curtailed, and there was little energy to answer the vast amounts of personal mail he received. Letters between Carver and Pickle ceased in 1938, and George W. Carver died on January 5, 1943.

In preparation for this book, I searched through many reference books, newspaper and magazine articles, and computer resources. A number of libraries, both public and academic, were visited and their archived computer records were searched for pertinent information. The George Washington Carver National Monument in Diamond, Missouri, and the G. W. Carver Museum and Archives at Tuskegee University in Tuskegee, Alabama, provided a great deal of information. The research library at Simpson College in Indianola, Iowa, and the Iowa State University Library and Special Collections Archives in Ames were also used. Finally, available letters between George W. Carver and "His Boy" Johnnie Pickle from 1932 until 1938 were transcribed for inclusion in this volume.

The reader who wants to learn more about George W. Carver and his amazing life will find abundant resources; in my "Resources" at the end, I have asterisked and annotated some books that I consider especially useful in detailing the life and travels of George W. Carver and providing significant information about this godly man of science.

My own book does not attempt to chronicle the life and times of George Washington Carver, since that has been done numerous times by others. Instead I direct the reader to interesting aspects of the famous Wizard of Tuskegee and the special influence and mentoring relationship that developed between him and my father.

As the oldest son of one of Carver's Boys, I believe Carver's positive influence, the miracle of his life, his skill, personality, and spiritual guidance, as well as the impact of his accomplishments, are still manifest within the children and grandchildren of those the great man reached directly throughout his life. It is obvious that Carver's impact on my father resonates in Johnnie Pickle's eight children and numerous grandchildren and great-grandchildren.

ACKNOWLEDGMENTS

I want to thank for their aid and guidance the many people who provided assistance, consultation, photographs, and documents utilized in this publication. Without them, this book would not have been possible.

I'd first like to thank Curtis Gregory of the George Washington Carver National Monument in Diamond, Missouri, for directing me to Gary R. Kremer's *In His Own Words*, the first reference book that led me to Carver's Boys. In addition, working with Dana Chandler and his staff in the George Washington Carver Museum at Tuskegee University has been very educational, inspirational, and significant in terms of this project.

I must also thank the special collections staff at Iowa State University: David A. Faux, Kimberly Anderson, and Dr. A. Deborah Lewis. Their assistance and help was much appreciated.

The library staff at Simpson College, especially Cynthia M. Dyer, were of great help, as was Debbie Zacharias of the Madison County Historical Society.

I wish to think Nancy Spencer and her staff at the Lodi Public Library in Lodi, Wisconsin, for searching for and providing the *American Magazine* article "A Boy who was Traded for a Horse" and the *Liberty* article "Black Man's Miracles."

I thank my wife, Beverly A. Baerwolf, for putting up with the books and files stacked all over the house while I read and researched for this book. I was a mess and a stacker and I know it pushed the limits of tolerance. Though not involved in the writing of *One of His Boys*, I would not have been able to accomplish this without her support.

My siblings assisted in the personal rewrites of the section on each of them and that was an unanticipated effort that they took on with gusto.

I want to give special thanks and appreciation to Matthew Byrne of NewSouth Books for all of his patience and proficiency in editing and making suggestions for this manuscript. Many thanks.

The authors who wrote about George W. Carver helped those of us who followed learn more about this amazing person. Authors such as Edwards, Elliott, Holt, Burchard,

Kremer, Hersey, Gart, and Clark each provided information that was extremely important in understanding the man and gaining insight into his purposes and goals. Librarians and researchers added depth of knowledge to the information. We are all in their debt.

Partial List of Boys

Thomas M. Campbell
Myrle Cooper
Austin W. Curtis Jr.
Howard Frazier
Wallace Fridy
James T. Hardwick
Cecil Johnson
Dana H. Johnson
_____ Lilly Jr.

John H. Pickle
Nathaniel Powell
Carl Reeves
Larry Robinson
A. I. Smith
Hubert Taylor Jr.
Asa Vaughn Jr.
Al Zissler

This list was compiled by the author from extant materials. There were far more boys than listed above, but their names were not available.

One of His Boys

Prologue:
My Father, Johnnie

One of His Boys features but one of many aspects of my father Johnnie Pickle's life: his relationship with Dr. George W. Carver, who mentored and guided Johnnie in letters and a few in-person meetings. Their fateful connection at the University of Mississippi sparked a remarkable friendship, and much of this book is devoted to their letters. But first, allow me to introduce you to my father.

John (Johnnie) Hornsby Pickle was born October 19, 1908, to William Woody Pickle and Francis (Fannie) Willis Basham Pickle. He was the youngest of seven children, with four sisters and two brothers, both of whom died prematurely.* Johnnie's mother ran the home and set

---

* Clifton, his eldest brother, died of influenza at the age of twenty-one in November of 1918 in Rio de Janeiro while serving his country in the Navy on the USS *Pittsburgh*. His second brother, James,

3

chores for the children. His father owned and operated a general store just outside Aberdeen, Mississippi, until the Great Depression destroyed the national economy, taking the Pickles' store and the local banks with it.

The family had only their large garden, a milk cow, a flock of chickens, and their strong backs to support themselves and share with friends. The family also had Johnnie's abilities as a hunter and fisherman to provide meat for the table. His affinity for and comfort in nature made Johnnie an able provider for his family, playing that role even as a teenager. When not working, he spent as much time as possible hunting, fishing, hiking, camping, and swimming. He was active in the Boy Scouts of America and earned his Eagle Scout rank as a young teen along with a Senior Lifesaving Certificate. In the summer, Johnnie worked as a lifeguard at the local swimming pool.

During his high school years, Johnnie and a couple of his friends spent time traveling to local fairs, where they boxed for money to earn spending cash. The three boys did quite well at these fairs. One would bet money that

---

also died at twenty-one from influenza complications stemming from his participation in a basketball game in 1922. Johnnie's sisters—Addine, Lorene, Fannie, and Allie B.—all lived to be near one hundred years of age, the latter three outliving their spouses.

he could stand with his arms to his side and both feet on a handkerchief and a combatant would not be able to hit him in the face. He won—usually. The other young man's father ran a horse-and-mule lot and he would bet that he could, with a single blow, knock the mule to its knees without causing any permanent damage. Johnnie was the boxer and would take on any challenger, others taking bets. He had very fast hands and a terrific left jab combined with a powerful hook with either hand. He rarely lost. After Johnnie won a fight against a professional boxer in Memphis, Tennessee, he was offered a lucrative boxing contract to go to Chicago and fight for a promoter. If he accepted, he was to receive $500 per week plus 10 percent of the gate. Because he was a good fighter, he considered the offer seriously and went for a second opinion from one of his favorite teachers. This teacher knew of Johnnie's skill but asked him if he would be willing to allow them to use his head as a punching bag without any medical assurances from the promoter. Then where would Johnnie be? After this, he opted to go to school.

Johnnie wanted to go to college and decided on the University of Mississippi for geology, despite not having money to go. He was accepted and played football at Ole Miss. Doctors could not repair an injury to his knee during his freshman year, and he struggled with that knee for the rest of his life. Johnnie had to work his way through college, but he still finished his bachelor's degree in three-and-a-half years, graduating in August of 1932. Earlier that year he met Carver, who would change his life.

1

Off to Meet the Wizard

*"In my work I meet many young people who
are seeking truth. God has given me some
knowledge. When they will let me, I try to pass
it on to my boys."*

GEORGE W. CARVER, speaking privately to
Jim Hardwick at the YMCA Blue Ridge
summer conference in 1922

In 1922 George W. Carver was a featured speaker at the
summer conference of the YMCA held in Blue Ridge,
North Carolina. Despite Carver's established reputation
as a famous scientist, researcher, and motivational speaker,
the young white men in attendance felt that he should not
have been allowed there. After Carver completed his talk,
however, many responded with enthusiasm and crowded
the podium to shake his hand and try to talk to him. One

of these admirers was Jim Hardwick, but he was not settled on his opinion of the man. Jim came from a Virginia family that had owned slaves to work their plantation prior to the Civil War. Due to this facet of his upbringing, Hardwick was still developing his perspective on the evolving state of race relations in the United States. In a private conversation that night, Carver asked him to become "one of his Boys." This bothered Hardwick, as he had rarely interacted so personally with people of color, and he backed away. However, since he did not understand the meaning of the question, he later went back to Carver and resumed their conversation. Hardwick asked Carver questions and skirted the issue until finally he just asked what the scientist meant about becoming "his Boy."

Meeting Hardwick that night, Carver recognized the struggle the young white man was going through. He could say with confidence at the age of fifty-eight that he had experienced much hardship in life and overcome it. If Hardwick would allow it, the famous George W. Carver would serve as a mentor in the young man's life, providing advice for any of Hardwick's concerns or struggles. The young man thought about this for a while and then decided that he would like to be "one of Carver's Boys."

Hardwick was the first of many who allowed Carver

to serve as his mentor. The relationship was, as Carver stated it, like Timothy was to St. Paul of the New Testament; the follower would help and assist in furthering the work of the leader. Carver called Jim Hardwick the first and number one Spiritual Boy. They accomplished much together, especially working jointly with the Young Men's Christian Association (YMCA) and the Commission on Interracial Cooperation (CIC). They worked to further racial and spiritual growth for the betterment of all. To be one of George Carver's Boys was by invitation only, and he looked for young men who had a Christian upbringing, were idealistic, had a college education, and were looking to make their place in society. It was a real privilege to be "one of his Boys."

JOHNNIE PICKLE MET THE famous George Washington Carver by accident in 1932 when he was asked by Ole Miss YMCA Secretary Malcolm Guess to serve as a guide for Carver. They were to search for diseased plants or geological props for Carver to use in his presentation for the YMCA-sponsored meeting that evening. Johnnie and Dr. Carver went into the fields near the University of Mississippi's campus looking for interesting things that could be used. Carver was sixty-eight and Johnnie only twenty-four years of age. Johnnie was good in the outdoor environment but Carver "blew him away" with his knowledge of nature and the familiarity that he had with each organism they came upon. Carver would see a plant, insect, or rock material, call it by its scientific name, and tell Johnnie its life cycle, uses, and special traits. Johnnie knew plants by their common name and he, being a geology major, knew the details of rocks and soil, but the degree of information Carver was providing on everything they saw as they were walking in the fields, woods, and creek bottoms amazed Pickle. As Carver was identifying and sharing information about the flora and fauna, he would quote scripture or poetry. The young white man accompanying him found this unique and strange. Johnnie had been raised in a Southern Baptist church, so hearing the Bible being quoted was not strange. It was hearing scripture and poetry recited in connection to nature that was unlike anything he had ever experienced. Johnnie was left very impressed.

That evening Johnnie went to the YMCA meeting to hear Dr. George Washington Carver's presentation. Upon introduction, the reception of Carver was tepid and most expected to be "bored to tears," because this was a Black man and these were white students. At first they politely listened with only limited interest. However, Carver delivered such a positive talk on science and religious inspiration that those in attendance became a vibrant, excited audience who cheered wildly at the end. Many rushed forward to shake Dr. Carver's hand at the conclusion of his speech and tell him how much they enjoyed it and wanted to learn more. Johnnie was in that group of excited admirers. He wanted to go to Tuskegee to see Carver's laboratory and talk more with this great man. This YMCA meeting occurred in April 1932. Johnnie was scheduled to complete his undergraduate degree in August of the same year, lacking only his final course and a few exams.

Johnnie did go to see Dr. Carver at Tuskegee and apparently spent three days with him conversing, walking in nature, asking questions, and looking at experiments. Carver had arranged lodging for the young man in Dorothy Hall, the Tuskegee Institute's guest house. Dr. Carver asked Johnnie if he would be "one of his Boys." My father indicated that he would like that, and over the course of the next few years Carver happily mentored Johnnie through some difficult times physically, spiritually, and emotionally. This all occurred in the days of the Great Depression and continued until the country started recovering from those trying times.

2

One of His Boys

The following account was written by Johnnie Pickle—and typed by his wife Katherine Scott Brown Pickle—in the 1970s in the hope that it would be published in *Reader's Digest*. He never completed the manuscript; nor did he submit it for publication. The draft read:

This is the story, as it is told often to anyone who would listen, of John Hornsby Pickle's friendship with Dr. George Washington Carver, the noted black scientist, and Dr. Carver's influence on John's life. John was born in Aberdeen, Mississippi, where he graduated from high school in June of 1929, the year of the stock market "crash" and the start of the Great Depression of the 1930s. John's father (Woody or W. W.) owned a small general store, which was located on the banks of the Tombigbee River a mile east of Aberdeen and just across U.S. Highway 45 from a big cotton gin. The cotton gin drew farmers and their helpers, both black and white, from the surrounding rich farmland, and while they waited for their turn at the cotton gin, they gathered at the Pickle store to talk about news of the day and to drink "Cokes." Woody knew everyone and it was his custom to let people buy on credit. With the arrival of the "Great Depression," money seemed to disappear, along with the jobs that earned the money, and the Pickle store was forced to close. The family survived with a large vegetable garden, a milk cow, and chickens that kept the family well fed and was shared with neighbors and friends. There was no money for Johnnie to attend college, and the only job he could find was as a lifeguard at the city swimming pool. Yet Johnnie was determined to go to school at "Ole Miss" and major in geology.

In the fall of 1929, Johnnie went to Oxford to see what he could do to earn his way to an education. He found many other young people with the same quest in mind. Dr. E. N. Lowe, a well-known geology professor, finally offered to let Johnnie sleep on a cot in his basement in exchange for keeping his furnace stoked with coal and doing other chores around the house. Dr. Lowe was also helpful in John's getting a job as a janitor of the geology building to earn money for tuition and books.

So John's dream of getting a college education began to be fulfilled. By attending summer school each summer, John earned his degree in three years, graduating at the end of the summer of 1932.

It was in the spring of 1932 that the opportunity to spend several hours walking and talking with Dr. George Washington Carver arose. This made a tremendous impact on John's life. This is the story as John told it:

"I will lift up mine eyes unto the hills, from whence cometh my help. My help cometh from the Lord, which made heaven and earth" (Psalms 121: 1–2). Quoted this strange old Negro as we walked through the fields and meadows surrounding Oxford, Mississippi, on that warm spring day.

I am not quite sure why Malcolm Guess, secretary of the campus YMCA at "Ole Miss," and under whose auspices Dr. Carver came to speak, chose me to be Dr. Carver's guide. I shall always be grateful for this inspiring experience. Mr. Guess knew that I enjoyed being in the out-of-doors and took walks in the woods whenever I could manage to get away from studies and work schedules.

I unintentionally called attention to myself when

a pet squirrel that I had raised from a baby caused an exasperated teacher to order me to leave his class. The squirrel lived in the dormitory room with me and had made a nest in my room-mate's hat. The room-mate did not object to this until the squirrel decided to use some of the room-mate's school papers for lining the nest. This resulted in my room-mate's strong suggestion that I not leave the squirrel in the room unattended. Since I did not know what to do with the squirrel, I put the squirrel in my inside coat pocket, where it was content to curl up and go to sleep, and I hurried to class. It was a rather dull class, and most of the students were half asleep, including the young lady seated at the desk just behind me. The squirrel got restless and started crawling around underneath my jacket, finally going around my waist and up my back and stuck his head out of my collar at the back of my neck. The young lady that was seated at the desk behind me opened her sleepy eyes, jumped to her feet, and let out a scream that could be heard over the entire building. Needless to say, the teacher ordered me and my squirrel from the room and threatened to have me expelled from school. Of course, the story was spread over the entire campus and I became quite famous as a lover of wildlife. The squirrel had to be taken to the woods and released, but perhaps this escapade had something to do with my being picked to be the guide for Dr. Carver.

The walk with Dr. Carver was like a day spent with God, where nature came to life and every single item took on new meaning.

"One has to be a master of things," he said as he pointed out a bird here, a wildflower there, and collected sticks with fungi on them.

"Do you kill sparrows and blue jays, which are pests?" I asked.

"Who are we to say that they are pests? God puts many things into the world and there develops a balance which will limit their spread," he said kindly.

"How do you remember all of these things, Dr. Carver?" I marveled.

"I don't remember them, Mr. Pickle. I make friends with them and you just don't forget real friends. You know them so well that they are part of you," he replied.

"Do you remember all the work you did in school?" I asked, thinking of final exams that were fast approaching. He laughed.

"Listen, my handsome boy, God has given you a creative mind, and you, too, will learn and remember. Learn each lesson well, condense it, and then go back over this material as often as you need to remember it. Once each year should be enough, and then it should become completely yours. In this way, you should know many things intimately."

All day long we went from one wonder to another, and I forgot that this was a Negro and I a Southern white boy. Here was a man of science with the faith of my mother in God, and believing that I could become a master of things, a true server of Him, who is the giver of all things.

That evening I heard him speak to the entire student body. I saw him change a curious, half-hearted audience into a moving, dynamic, pulsing body. The students sat in rapt attention. I don't know how many students remember that talk, but it was the beginning of an epoch of my life.

After Dr. Carver left to return to Tuskegee, I was to make one of the most important decisions of my life. There were still no jobs available, even for college graduates. Now that I was approaching graduation, where should I go from here? Dr. E. N. Lowe, my beloved geology professor, whose health was failing, asked me if I would be interested in staying at "Ole Miss" the next year to help him with the geology department. It was a big temptation to stay, yet there was a stirring in me, an unrest, a

quest of something that I must follow. I wrote to Dr.
Carver and asked him if he still wanted me to visit him.
He answered my letter the day he received it.

8-8-32

My beloved boy Mr. Pickle:

Fine, come right on. I will be here except for a few
hours only one day this week, when I must go to the
Capitol City, to meet with the Gov. and the highway man
who are interested in the cotton seed building blocks.

I will be right back. I am so glad you are coming.
"Where there is no vision, the people perish." "To be
sure, many people cannot see what you see, never will."

There are quite a number of persons who would
not be benefitted at all by coming. Not so with my dear
handsome boy "Johnnie." Will save the rest till you come.

Admiringly yours,

G. W. Carver

When Dr. Carver's letter arrived the next week assuring
me that I was still welcome to visit him, I knew that I
would have to hitch-hike to Tuskegee, since I had no
money. I went with some misgivings. Here I was, a
Southern white boy who had grown up in a small town

on the edge of the "black prairie belt" where half of the
population was black. Blacks and whites lived in separate
parts of town, went to separate schools and churches, ate
in different restaurants. White families often had black
cooks, nurse-maids, or gardeners but blacks and whites
lived segregated lives. For a white person to visit a Negro,
if not unheard of, it certainly wasn't mentioned.

I need not have thought of it at all! Dr. Carver was
as smart as he was kind. He would be the last one in the
world to let anyone make a step which might embarrass
himself. He had a special room set up for me with service
fit for a king. Always his manner was courteous and kind.
He didn't have to put on a single "high-brow air" to let
you know that he was a gentleman and a Great Man in
every sense of the word.

The days at Tuskegee were over far too soon. After
much discussion and soul-searching I had resolved to
go to graduate school to try to find what I was seeking.
As strange as it may seem, I decided that since I had no
money for going to school, I would choose the school
I wanted to attend and go. I chose the University of
Wisconsin, because of the excellent reputation of the
geology department.

As I bid farewell to Dr. Carver and thanked him for

his faith in me, he gave me an envelope and told me not to open it until I was well on my way. I made my way to the highway to try to catch a ride toward home. When I opened the envelope that Dr. Carver had given me, there was a five-dollar bill along with this message:

8-10-32

My beloved boy Mr. Pickle:

This is to let you know further what a great joy it was to have had you with me. It was a real benediction, as I have confirmed what I saw at the university. Take care of your splendid physique and your creative mind.

I trust that I shall always have the privilege of keeping in touch with you. Somehow, in some way, I feel that God is going to arrange it so that you can come back at some future time.

To me, you are the ideal young man from every angle. You make me happy all of the time.

Yours with love and admiration,

G. W. Carver

P. S. Dear, you need never to mention the little enclosure. I want you to get certain little comforts you may need on the way, and if you get tired take the train or bus. My prayers for your safe arrival shall follow you all the way.

I am so happy over my dear handsome boy "Johnnie."
Don't expose yourself to bad weather; take the train or
bus if the weather gets bad.

I soon caught a ride as far as Birmingham. Unable to
get a ride any farther, I walked to the railroad tracks
and climbed aboard a freight train going to Columbus,
Mississippi, which was only twenty-five miles from my
hometown, Aberdeen. Riding on a coal-fired freight
train left me covered with soot and cinders, and I didn't
want my mother to see me looking so dirty. Also my
appearance might keep me from being able to catch
a ride on home, so I bathed in a creek and continued
my way home. I wrote Dr. Carver a note to thank him
for his kindness to me. Promptly his reply came back,
thanking me for coming.

8-15-32
My beloved boy Mr. Pickle:
    Dear, your card reached me Sun. morning and your
greetings, it was so good for you to let me know that you
arrived home safely.
    My dear boy "Johnnie," just like all of my other
precious boys, they don't seem to mind very well. I was

just hoping that you would say nothing about the little enclosure. I just wanted my dear handsome boy to have a little extra to get a few comforts if he needed them.

I am confident you are going to build upon it. I am now looking forward to the time when you can come again. You only saw a few things this time. You will see many others when you come back. I want you to know that to me you are just my idea of an ideal young man, from every angle. Some day you will be the head of some group of research . . . so that such a . . . are . . . .

I am not at all disturbed . . . , you have the creative instincts to develop some of it when I see you again. . . . feel that I must have my precious boy long enough to get him started in something, so that he can go on developing. My daily prayers shall follow you. Mrs. Owens and the others enjoyed you very much.

With so much love and admiration, I am sincerely yours.

G. W. Carver

And now—the big step. The country boy, who had never been farther north than Reelfoot Lake (Tennessee), wanted to go to school in Wisconsin, and with no money! With a full sense of desperation—everything to gain and nothing to lose. (Dr. Carver had started from nothing, and so could I.) I started out with five dollars in my pocket. God was good to me! I reached Madison on Sunday afternoon, August 22, 1932, with thirty-seven cents in my pocket. I didn't know anyone nearer than Memphis, Tennessee, and I had no idea where to go. I found my way to the Madison YMCA, and left my suitcase; then, I started walking. I am sure that God directed me. I walked in the exact opposite direction from the university campus, along the midway and toward the Northwestern Railway Depot. Along the way I spotted a busy little restaurant, Cleveland's Lunch, and stopped to get a piece of pie and a glass of milk. It was a warm, friendly place and people from all walks of life seemed to patronize the place. I introduced myself to the manager, Leonard Nelson, and asked him about the possibility of my getting a job there in exchange for my meals. He replied "your chances are pretty good. The two boys who were here last year won't be back. See Bill Anderson, the owner, in the morning about six o'clock and you might get on." Of course my Southern accent attracted a lot of attention and everyone laughed each time I opened my mouth to speak.

I left Cleveland's Lunch with hope in my heart and

a prayer on my lips. In my wanderings I discovered the path along beautiful Lake Mendota, which borders on the northern edge of the business district, and as I walked beside the lake, I prayed for guidance. About ten o'clock I went back to the YMCA and asked Mr. Best, the night clerk, for some newspapers. I had decided that I would have to sleep outside, perhaps beside the lake. But Mr. Best, being the kindly, wise old man that he was, asked me where I was going to spend the night. I replied that I planned to spend the night in the park, since I didn't have any money.

"Would you like to sweep the lobby for your room tonight?" he asked. All over America there are men like this, with compassion in their hearts, yet with empathy to let a man save his pride. Of course, I swept the lobby, as many other young men have done, smugly innocent and thinking that I had really earned my room for the night. Gratefully, I left a request to be called the next morning in time to be at Cleveland's Lunch, before six o'clock. I wanted to be sure that the chance to earn my meals did not pass me by.

Even though I had no restaurant experience, Bill Anderson agreed to hire me on a two-week trial basis. He must have seen the hungry look in my eyes! Since I had to walk everywhere I went, I kept hoping that I could find work closer to the university, rather than all the way across town. I would search for other work later. Right now I was grateful to have a job where I could earn my meals. When I wasn't waiting on customers, I would polish sugar-shakers, or give the counter an extra wiping, or help any way I could. I listened to the special "lingo" of the other workers in the restaurant and watched to see what the customer got from these strange orders, and I learned. I began to feel more secure in my job.

Now that my meals were taken care of, I needed to make some permanent arrangements for a place to live. I went back to the YMCA and talked to Don Newton, the boy's program director. When he found out that I knew how to teach swimming, he offered me a job teaching swimming to pay for my room. Who would have thought that those earlier summers teaching swimming and serving as a lifeguard in the home-town pool would be such an asset to my livelihood now?

I still needed a job to earn money for school expenses, so I began my search, around the square, up one side of State Street and down the other. No one could afford any help. Then came the crushing blow . . . I could not enroll at the university because the out-of-state tuition was $100 per semester. I had never in my life had that much money at one time! The registrar thought I was crazy. He said "Why don't you go back to Mississippi where you belong? Don't you know a man can't go to school without any money?" Disappointment and frustration overwhelmed me and I snapped back at the registrar, "I didn't come to ask you what I can't do! I came to ask what I can do!"

If I hadn't been so desperate for an education, I would have gone home then. Instead, I went to the Dane County Court House and registered to vote. I would establish residence in Wisconsin, so that I would not have to pay out-of-state tuition. This meant that I would have to wait a year to enter the university. One year from September 13, 1932, I would legally be a resident of the state of Wisconsin.

Bill Anderson agreed to keep me working at Cleveland's Lunch and since I never watched the clock and worked overtime whenever help was needed, he often paid me cash for overtime, money sorely needed and the most precious dollars of my life.

During the next year, I barely existed. Hard, bitter experiences were mine. During this trying time I gave up many precious things. I drew within myself to such an extent that I wanted no one to have to share the humiliating experiences of not being able to overcome a situation. But I came to go to school, and unless God deemed otherwise, I was going! Through these turbulent days, Dr. Carver was a constant inspiration and his letters and those from my mother were all that kept me trying!

9-27-32

My beloved boy, Mr. Pickle:

Dear, your fine letter comes as such a welcome messenger. I am so happy to hear from my precious boy "Johnnie." I never cease to think of and pray for you. There is much in prayer, note the history of Mr. Gandhi through prayer.

I am so happy for you. God seems to be unusually well providing in these puzzling times. "In all thy ways acknowledge him and he will direct thy paths." It seems dear, that your paths have been directed so far. Remember a devoted boy's mother is lifting her voice up to God for her boy all the time. God will hear her.

Fine, if you can take any or all of those extra courses, do so. You will need them, no difference when in a career, in the future. I am not worried that my dear handsome boy Johnnie Pickle will be a great versatile scholar that will fit him for great needs in the world.

I hope that you read an article in the Oct. issue of

the American Magazine by J. S. Childers. I think you know the individual he has written about.

Dear, I thought about you this morning. I went out about seven miles from here collecting. My, what a marvelous time I had. I came back loaded down with specimens.

You certainly were thinking straight when you established residence there. You have exactly my idea for you. O yes, you must not only do all you say but more. I must have my precious boy again. No dear, I do not consider that you are just floundering around, you are getting somewhere with it. Creative minds do just that. I am expecting so much out of my dear boy "Johnnie." Yes, stay single until your education is finished.

May God bless, keep and direct you. Provide for you also.

Admiringly yours,

G. W. Carver

In October, I was despondent and soul-searching and wrote to Dr. Carver, knowing that his letters to me were always an inspiration. His long reply to me indicated that he felt I needed help. I wrote to him and he responded rapidly.

10-19-32

Dear Dr. Carver,

In vocational school I am helping teach a chemistry course, beginner's chemistry, and it is a wonderful review for me. Soon I am to give a little talk to make chemistry more alive and real to them, to see the proactive side of it and to learn the wholesome joy of the desire (at least) to create new things. I wonder if I would talk about you, your work and methods—would you mind? I would like to tell them just how you approached the peanut, asking "What is the peanut?" "Why was it made?" "How can it be made use of?" and through your verses from the Bible, "Behold I have given you every herb—and to you it shall be meat." Then I'd like to know all the constituents of the peanut so I could show how each was extracted and then synthesized into new and wholesome products. Please, Dr. Carver, what are all of the constituents of the peanut? You said them so fast that I got only a few like amino acids, peptones, lactose, protein, etc. I'd like to go on showing that education was in knowing and seeing relations through association. The fourth kingdom, the synthetic kingdom and the law of compatibility, and try to get them to desire knowledge so that they would repent too, as I have done from hearing you, "Open thou mine eyes that I might behold the wondrous things of thy creation." I know I can never hope to present it as attractively and as well as you did, but if you don't mind, I'd like to try at least to get one to aspire to your work. At the very least chemistry will seem more alive and with soul after you have touched them.

Dr. Carver, I have no desire to be a great scholar, but I do hope that, some day, I can become master of things; to know those things that I come in contact with and to use them towards a better end of the human race. If I can ease a few peoples' pain and bring laughter where there was suffering; bring hope and faith and an altruistic outlook where there was blankness. If, in my meager way, I could do one-tenth of what you have done, then I don't think that I will have lived in vain. But at the same time I don't want to waste my time in blind blunderings and lost motion. In swimming, I try to teach that one stroke correctly executed gets one further than floundering motion, and saves lots of energy. I hope that I can apply that to my life. You know, Dr. Carver, I have to watch myself, else I would be perpetually talking to you and wasting your time. If I wrote you every time I thought of you, there would be a continuous string of letters pouring in to you.

The people here in the North cannot understand why I, a full-blooded Southerner, should be so crazy about you. But I have only one answer for that, the educated classes of both white and colored know that the only way that the race question will ever be settled is to raise humanity above the narrow, self-imprisoned barriers of race. Honestly and frankly, I know no man anywhere who I admire more than I do you. You exemplify all that I have ever held in my dreams as pure, unselfish and big to me. When a man's a man, we don't think so much who he is, but what he is. He can and should do worlds for people as you have done and are doing.

I could rave on hours and hours to you, Dr. Carver, and about you, but try to understand that I mean well, even if I am awkward, and all I am trying to say is that I love you and all you stand for.

One of your Boys,

Johnnie Pickle

P.S. I have read the article in the Oct. American not once but many times. My birthday was Oct. 10th and I honestly felt that article was a present to me.

What do you think of Madison sewage disposal plants? Isn't human refuse fertilizer, a very rich fertilizer? Aren't we wasting millions of dollars on commercial fertilizer when we could be using human manure and waste water? Tell me how to approach it? What do I look for in the constituents for the sewage waste water and how to get what has been done on the subject? I am going out to the Madison disposal plant as soon as I can, in hopes to see what they are doing. The plant is about five miles from town, but I'll walk pretty soon if I don't find a way out there. It's raining now though.

I'll stay single a long time and maybe longer. The height of mere ambition is to spend a while with you and learn to attack individual problems.

Sincerely yours,

Johnnie P.

10-21-32

My very own precious boy, Mr. Pickle,

Your wonderful letter has reached me, I say wonderful advisedly, as you are one of my dear, dear little family of boys whom God has laid his hand. I am very certain that you are well aware that God picked you out and gave you to me there in Miss., just as He gave little Timothy to Paul, used indeed for much the same purpose.

You are right, many cannot see what you see. I

have the same thing to endure from my own people. They cannot understand why I have white people always hanging around me, as they call it. I consider it a compliment. Anyone who cannot get away from self, sufficiently far to see the God in man, regardless of nationality, complexion or religious belief, cannot . . . , because they are quite positively, absurd to me. I love them because God speaks to me through them. I loved you from the very moment my eyes fell upon you as Mr. Hardwick will testify. I told him about you before I had ever spoken to you.

Dear, I think that God made it possible for you to have such wonderful opportunities for development, right along the lines that are going to fit into the development of your creative mind. I wish I had a person now to send to Mexico to take care of the millions of coconuts that are rotting down there and people are starving. They have appealed to me for help, I cannot possibly do it. Had I the time, I could work out many products for them. By and by my precious boy Johnnie will be able to take some of these things. I have dozens and dozens of them before me all the time.

Dear, I like your idea about sewage. I am quite sure you are right. In some of the Oriental countries it is used for fertilizer purposes. It would be important to get an analysis and find out definitely its value as a fertilizer.

Dear, under a separate cover I am sending you "Bul. 31" on peanuts, in it you will find the composition. Of course you already know about the fats, oils, etc. Their composition of fatty acids and glycerides, amino acids come in also with azachin, conorachin and legume. Arrange these dear as you like in your talk. What he is, as you say, is so much more than who he is.

I doubt if a magazine article has come out within the last few years that has attracted as much attention as Mr. Childress's article in the American Magazine. Hundreds of letters are coming to me about it. Some of the most beautiful I have ever seen, some very touching.

I have just returned from Phila., Penn., Washington, D.C. and Danville, Virginia, where I went to inspect a plant's bottling works etc., where my product Penol will be manufactured. This laboratory in Phila. covers 10 acres and employs nearly 3,000 people. How I wish I could have had my precious boy Johnnie with me.

I will pray for my dear boy. I know you will do well, as you have a pretty voice and a pleasing personality. I know you will bring a new vision to your success. I shall be intensely interested in how you come out. With so

much love and admiration for my very own precious
boy, Johnnie Pickle,

    G. W. Carver

Dr. Carver always answered a letter on the day he received
it, and for that reason, I never wrote very often. He was
in demand for so many things, all of them very important. I was hesitant about his using his valuable time to
answer my letters.

I sent him a Christmas card at Christmas time in 1932.
He responded with a letter and enclosed a small painting
that he had done, using the native Alabama clays he dug
from the hills around Tuskegee. It was from these clays
that he developed the many lovely and inexpensive paints
for painting houses around that part of the country. He
was also a talented artist and used some of his paints to
paint pictures, which he gave to friends and showed in
art exhibits.

12-25-32

My beloved boy, Mr. Pickle:

How happy I was to get the beautiful card with its choice greeting. But above all that was the poem written by your own hands.

I thank God every day that our paths met. I am enclosing a little card which I am sure my precious boy will like, as you are interested in clays.

With the hope that the New Year will bring to you many additional joys and successes.

Yours with so much love and admiration, looking forward to the time when I can have you with me again.

G. W. Carver

P.S. See the coloring on this card was made from clay.

Card gifted to Johnnie by Carver for Christmas, 1932

1-18-33

Dear Dr. Carver,

I was and am very proud of the little card you sent me. It will always be a constant reminder to me of the greatest character that I know and as an inspiration to keep digging. Sometimes I almost wished that I could be handicapped in some way so that my interest would not be torn so much.

I have been sick with cold and flu quite a bit this year and between that and digging for existence I have neglected the work I like best to do. I guess the first necessity of life is to live and better if he can and let live.

The days are flying by so fast that I hardly know when they come and go. The only thing that I have been able to do constantly is to make someone a little happier each day. That is very easy and I know quite a few children and old people here already, but my study and so called mental improvements may or may not be. I have not yet become a master of things as you have and I so much desire to be. There is the most wonderful flower shop and green house here. One lily I notice, a great white cup shaped one; maybe you know it—an Egyptian lily—Lilaceae ethiopica.

I am trying to start a war on sparrows, English

sparrows, to permit our songbirds back to the cities. I wonder at the justice of this to the sparrow, but at the same time I can see the relentless march of the little street gamins [sic] and the expulsion of our songbirds, to out of the way places. What do you think about it?

Dr. Carver, I won't be hypocritic [sic] enough to say that I'll be any one thing in life, but I can promise you one thing and that is, regardless of where I am or what I'm doing, I'll always try to brighten that little spot wherever I may be. The lessons that you have taught me are among the most wonderful of my life and I won't let them stop.

Are you still working on plant diseases and control? Are you painting any? I could ask you a thousand questions, but I won't be so selfish in that.

Of all things good, I know of none better than to be with you again. Although the contact was small, the seeds you planted were fertile. I hope that I can make success in cultivating the ground.

Your devoted friend and disciple,

Johnnie Pickle

Dr. Carver had very little social life. His work schedule was too demanding. But he was usually the guest of some of the Tuskegee staff on special holidays. Otherwise his laboratory and experiment station filled his life, and he seemed to shrink from anything that would have made it any different.

In Lawrence Elliott's biography, *George Washington Carver: The Man Who Overcame,* the story is told of one Christmas evening in the Tom Campbell home, when Dr. Carver "lost himself in play with the Campbell children, one of which was named for him. Dr. Carver had brought them a top-like toy that he had made for them, and while the children howled with glee—and Dr. Carver cackled triumphantly—spinning it again and again, crawling under the tree to retrieve it and spinning it once more. Later seated on the sofa with a child on each knee, he told them a story about a little boy who could talk with the flowers."

After the children were tucked into bed, young Mrs. Campbell said softly, "You have a good way with children, Professor Carver. You ought to have a family of your own." He smiled as he replied. "What woman would want a husband forever dropping soil specimens all over her parlor? How could I explain to a wife that I had to go out at four o'clock every morning to talk to the flowers?" "Oh, the right woman would understand," assured Mrs. Campbell.

But Dr. Carver never married; however, there was one young woman, Sarah Hunt, that he must have cared for very deeply. She was a teacher in the fourth grade in the university school, at Tuskegee. Small, pert and vivacious, she was attracted to Dr. Carver by his dedication and talents. They were seen sharing conversation at meal times in the cafeteria and as they walked across campus sharing animated talks or magically, shared silence. It did not last long. Dr. Carver was past forty years old and if he was to marry, it must be now and to this girl. But it was not to be. Dr. Carver had dedicated himself to his work of helping others. It was not fair to expect a wife to stand by, while he continued his life of dedication. He needed to continue his life as it was—rising at four each morning to talk with God and go for his walk in the woods, teaching his classes, conducting his research in the laboratory, massaging the polio victims who came to him each day, taking his school on wheels to the farmers each weekend, teaching his Bible class each Sunday night, going on speaking tours to colleges and high schools in the surrounding area. There was no time for family life.

Perhaps it was this realization that brought about Dr. Carver's search for "His Boys." He knew that he would never have any children of his own, so he began to use his own tremendous spiritual awareness to pick out highly motivated, idealistic young men, who had a strong religious faith, and "adopt" them as his own.

Glenn Clark, who wrote *The Man Who Talks With Flowers,* one of the first short biographies of Dr. Carver, tells the story of how Jim Hardwick, former football player and later an ordained minister, became one of Dr. Carver's boys. Mr. Clark went to hear Jim Hardwick speak. "The moment he began to speak with that soft Virginia drawl of his, there awoke romantic echoes in every youthful heart within hearing distance. It was like picking one's way down a gunflint trail toward inviting sunsets when Jim began speaking of the power of prayer. Everywhere he went he left changed lives behind him. I rarely have met a man, in all my going and coming across the continent, who could inspire young men and women who were earnestly seeking God, as Jim could.

"One day I asked Jim how he came by this hidden power of his. 'From an old Negro in Alabama,' was his instant reply. 'An old Negro?' I exclaimed! 'It was the most amazing experience of my life,' he continued. 'Have you ever heard of George Washington Carver of Tuskegee? One day he came to the town where I lived and gave an address on his discoveries of the peanut. I went to the lecture to learn science and came away knowing more about prayer than I had ever learned in the theological schools. And to cap the climax, when the old gentleman was leaving the hall, he turned to me, where I stood transfixed and inspired, and said, "I want you to be one of my boys." That is the way it began.'

"'You must have felt honored by his selecting you out of the rest of the audience that way.' 'No,' drawled Jim, 'just the opposite. It came very nearly spoiling the lecture. My grandfathers were owners of slaves. I came naturally by a strong Southern prejudice against the Negro. For a nigger to assume the right of adopting me into his family—even his spiritual family, as it was in this case—was brazen effrontery to my pride. I recoiled from it. So I went back to my room and tried to remove Dr. Carver entirely out of my mind. But try as I would, I could not erase the effect of the lecture. A few evenings later when I seriously needed help, almost unconsciously, I found myself turning thought to this genteel old scientist who had found God in the hills and fields and it seemed that his spirit filled the room. And his spirit was white, mind you, as white as any saint's in heaven. A peace entered me, and my problems fell away. Since then I have found that merely by turning in thought to that dear old gentleman, creates an atmosphere about which God can come very, very near to me. That is why God is as close to me as He is now.'"

No one really knew how many young men Dr. Carver called "his boys," but in 1932 Jim Hardwick wrote to as many as he could locate to ask each one to write a letter of appreciation to Dr. Carver, but to send it to Jim Hardwick, so he could have the letters bound in book form to present to Dr. Carver. This is the letter that I wrote:

Dear Dr. Carver,

It is my great pleasure to greet you as one of "your boys." I hope that in time I may prove worthy of your friendship and guidance to me. I have had many inspiring teachers and friends, but you, most of all have made my heart burn with the desire to do my bit for the good of the world. You and my mother have the deepest and broadest faith in God that I have ever seen. From the two of you I hope to catch the spark and spread it as you have done. Kant says that there is nothing good but a good will. That is true in that all humans are fallible, and some of your great creative work may die in time, but the spark of creative thinking and the goodwill that you have awakened in your boys will never die. It will grow and

accumulate force. And who knows but that your great
heart has solved the problem, not only of the South, but
of all the world and future generations that are to come! I
do not know, but I do know that your whole loving soul
to me is love itself. If I were precise in the manipulation
of making my soul, I would make an exact duplicate of
yours. You have shown me one race, the human race.
Color of skin or form of hair mean nothing to me now,
but the length and width and breadth of soul and loving
kindness mean everything. Won't you, as you read this,
send up a little prayer for me that I may grow broad and
deep in my love and understanding of men. My heart
surges with the desire to tell you what you have meant to
me. If I were a rose, I would bloom a deeper red for you;
but being only human, I linger with you for a moment
as I pray that God will always help me to keep fit, and
help me remain worthy in body and soul and purpose
and action to be one of your boys.

Most sincerely yours,

Johnnie Pickle*

---

*   This is, to the author's knowledge, the only surviving letter of those
included in a Remembrance book gifted to Carver that consisted
of letters from each of his Boys.

As soon as Dr. Carver was presented the book of letters he wrote this reply.

1-21-33

My beloved boy, Mr. Pickle:

A letter from my precious boy. How I wish you could understand what I meant by precious boy. It means just what Paul meant when he met dear little handsome Timothy in whom he saw, as you have marvelously said "only the human race" that Christ died to save. Paul was then an old man and he saw in his dear sweet little fellow the extension of the work that God had given him to do. He loved dear little Timothy so, that he called him his son. I love my boys in the same way.

Dear, I am sorry that you have had the flu. I have had the same thing and am not through with it yet.

Yes dear, we must live and let live, thus tried that day is here now. Only the strong mentally, morally and spiritually will be able to hear us out. My dear little family of boys must be the pioneers. 1933 to my mind is going to be the really hard year, the "decisive" year. Banks are still failing. On New Year Day, our only bank in town closed its doors, people are just frantic. It did not leave me with enough to get a pair of shoes. I am not suffering nor brooding over it. I am thanking God for a reasonable amount of heart strength and a job. With these I will make it. Yes dear, you have the true philosophy of hope to make people a little happier each day, some are helpless. They don't know what to do.

One of my table mates works most of the time because she lost in the bank. I tell her, to cheer up, go ahead, she and her husband both have jobs.

I am so glad that my precious boy loves flowers and nature. I do not have the lily of which you speak. It is rather rare and I have never seen it. My Amaryllis are just beginning to bud up nicely. In about a month they will be gorgeous. They are of my own breeding.

Dear, in all thy words, acknowledge him and he shall direct thy paths, would the song birds return, if it were possible to destroy all the sparrows? I was wondering if the song birds like city life? Let God decide this for you. I shall pray for guidance for my dear handsome boy.

No my boy is the "true blue," not a hypocrite from any angle whatsoever. You, with others of my precious little family are going to help the World of its present chaotic state, as fast as God gives you light and strength. Yes sir, I must have my precious boy again and again. You must see that wonderful testimonial book. In all my life I have never seen anything more expressive. It is a work of art, but above that it is the finest example of crystalized love I have ever seen. The book is priceless. It contains 46 letters. Your letter takes the prize. I let people read, not to coach them, and they pick out yours every time.

Glad you like the little painting. We will do many things when I can get my precious boy again. Dear, develop your fine creative mind as much as possible. Every day problems are coming to me, great problems, that I cannot think of touching.

Thanking God many, many times per day for my precious boy who has made me so very happy.

I am admiringly yours,

G. W. Carver

3

Metamorphosis of His Boy Johnnie

The account provided by Johnnie himself has been presented earlier in this volume. However, to achieve a full understanding of this mentorship, the remaining letters must be presented. Unfortunately letters are missing, causing interruptions in sequence, and words have been excised by rodent damage. Despite these challenges, a story can be told. As we fill in the gaps that my father left in his original manuscript, we must move back toward the beginning of the story.

When Professor Carver left Oxford, Mississippi, to return to Tuskegee, Johnnie penned a couple of letters to the professor expressing his thanks for the privilege of meeting Carver and for the religious experience in nature directed by Carver. Apparently there were two early letters that were never found in the Tuskegee Institute Archives and therefore we can only attempt to extrapolate possible statements in Johnnie's letters. Carver's responses are available.

Carver mentioned in 1932 the addition of new Boys to Jimmie Hardwick, his "first and Spiritual Boy."

6-16-32

My great spiritual boy, Mr. Hardwick:

You seemed to have been with me all day long today. I was conscious of your great spirit. In fact, dear, it has never left me since we made our triumphal march with God through Mississippi.

I also have before me a wonderful letter from the dear little boy, A. I. White who rode out to the Teacher's College in Hattiesburg. . . . I hear from Mr. Pickle right along also.

With much love and admiration.

G. W. Carver

6-26-32

My great spiritual boy, Mr. Hardwick;

The copy of letter which I inclose [sic] will show you why I have been so happy the last several days . . . I hear right along from the dear little boy we met in Hattiesburg, Johnnie Pickle and Mr. Lilly, the crippled boy.

Just had a letter from him yesterday . . . .

Yours with so much love and admiration.

G. W. Carver

6-16-32

Dear Dr. Carver,

Just finished my application for a degree this summer. Somehow just a B.A. degree seems very small and I'll certainly be glad when I learn enough to get a Dr.'s degree. This had been a very busy week for me, and a most interesting one. Yesterday, I classified my first flower, and it was a thrill to know that it was mine and that I would always be able to find it as a friend. It was one of the mint family, Monardi fistulosa. I know that you have experienced that same thrill, time and time again, as accomplishment assures itself.

You asked in one of your last letters if I would have the opportunity to use the microscope this summer. I am already using one a little, but have not drawn anything yet. Is it best to draw and attempt to classify everything one looks at through the microscope?

Dr. Carver, I'll have to confess that I waste quite a bit of time. There is a girl here I like very much, and who is making a special study of sciences, especially chemistry.

She plans to major in chemistry, although she was only a freshman last year. Frankly, do you think a person has the right to think about a girl when he plans to devote his life to science? Would it be fair to her? I've wondered about that quite a bit.

I've got something else I've wanted to ask someone and until you—had found no one I tho't was broad enough to judge. We mentioned religion while we were walking in the woods, but never got strung out on it. I have a peculiar religion—all my own; have never seen or heard anyone that had one like it. Here it is: I believe there is a Supreme Being, but have no idea as to shape, form or kind of existence. I think Jesus Christ was real but that it was love that was the true Son of God; I think Mohammed, Confucius and all the great men who have let Love rule their lives were also Sons of God. I think the Bible is true only in principle, and not necessarily in recording of instance and facts. I think some of those facts are true, but not all. I think that the secret of the Bible is that it is not to give us these great unchanging principles and think that many other books, deeds, lives and incidents give these same principles. When the Bible says—"He shall come again", I think that it means each of us has a chance to see real love for humanity and when we do personify that we shall live in love for all—that we have truly seen the return of Jesus Christ, and I think that is the only way we shall ever see them on earth. (Vague here—what I am trying to say is that to me Jesus Christ is love.) I think those people, whether they have seen the Bible or not, whether they've heard of Jesus Christ or not, who let live thus, live in love and service of their fellow man is a saved person, and if he does not do that regardless of what he swears to or believes, he is doomed to the land "of the forgotten." I think evil wears off in two or three generations, but that the great proponent of love will seem good down through generation after generation. Even now I am rather hazy as to the exact specifications of what I do believe. I find my religion changes with environment and conditions to fit the great principles that I fully believe were established by the Supreme One. Tell me what you think, won't you?

I watch and wait for the "scrawly" writing that I have grown to love. May I grow until I can catch the love that dominates your life and make it a fundamental fiber of my own being.

Your friend,

Johnnie Pickle

PROFESSOR CARVER WAS PROUD of finding new young men that he could mentor as his Boys. Johnnie Pickle was excited to be able to try to go see the great professor in Tuskegee and they must have exchanged letters stating that. Johnnie was also asking him for advice as to classes and schooling that he could consider. Johnnie's thoughts on religion were not in the mainstream of his home church in Aberdeen, the Baptist church (Primitive Southern Baptist). This young man, as with many youth, was attempting to find a way to express his internal religious beliefs and figure out how to practice those beliefs in his everyday life.

7-20-32

Dearest Dr. Carver,

I got your fine letter, and chemistry leaflet, and sure do appreciate them. It is the home lap for the first little race now. Examinations start Monday for me and will finish on the 29th. Have all of my flowers and about 10 over, but have about 20 of the 60 that I haven't classified yet. But will get them finished today and tomorrow. Was fortunate in finding 2 specimens of Blazing Star in one day—Liatris squarrosim and L. spicata. Am liking botany more and more, but am not spending as much time as I should on it.

Dr. Carver, it has been the hardest summer to accomplish anything that I have ever seen. Women and work just won't mix, and if I thought the next three years I would do as little work as I have done this summer, I would let her go—even as much as I love her. It has been a pleasant summer, but the kind that one looks back on and says: "yes, it was great but what have I done?" This summer has made me see the profoundness of the little phrase, "Men do not lack purpose, they lack will." I have the purpose but haven't the will, as much as I should. There are things I will never do but I do want to live a constructive life, like yours, so that when it is done I can look back and see things that I have planted, serving the world and making the lot of men better. Whether it is best to do this through science or through contact—I don't know, but I am going to work and follow your plan.

Remember these—I do

"In all thy ways acknowledge Him and He will direct thy path."

"Behold I will give you every herb and to you it shall be meat."

"I can do all things thru Christ who strengthen me."

"Open thou mine eyes that I might behold the wonders of thy Creation."

Sincerely yours.

Johnnie Pickle

P.S. Tell me what you honestly think of her. I think I am broad enough to take the criticism on criticism's worth. Thanks.

JOHNNIE WAS ROMANTICALLY SERIOUS about a fellow student and was questioning his mentor about if he should devote more time to his work, considering the economy and his career goals. Johnnie wanted Dr. Carver's opinion and advice on love, religious beliefs, and studies since he had some decisions to make in a few days. (In typical Carver fashion, he would not answer the question directly but would ask a question back and try to get Johnnie to answer his own question, a process termed Socratic questioning. It works well, as the student better retains what they have learned.)

At the end of the summer in 1932 Johnnie graduated from Ole Miss with a bachelor's degree in geology; however, there were no jobs available, as the Great Depression was in full force, and many young people continued their schooling in the hope that the job market would return in a few years. The following letter from Johnnie to Professor Carver indicates that they had been writing about options for Johnnie. A visit to Tuskegee was discussed and Johnnie decided that he would make the trip even though he would have to hitchhike to get there.

8-6-32

Dear Dr. Carver,

I am not a graduate, even if I did get my sheep skin. I'm just a foolish, ignorant, curious kid and want very much to see you, your laboratory and some of your work. I hope that by the time this reaches you that I will be with you. I hoped and prayed for a way to go, and none came. Now I'm going unless God wills it otherwise. Next week I plan to leave for Wisconsin, but I felt that I would be leaving the most precious thing in life, if I should lose the opportunity to be with you, even if it were only a day. I hope that I won't inconvenience you. I just had to come—now or maybe never.

You were right, I was extremely foolish to let myself fall in love. She is a wonderful girl, but she unconsciously hurts my hope to do work. She wouldn't do a thing to hinder and everything to help but she objects to the way I've got to travel. She doesn't yet realize that I don't go that way of want, but of necessity. I promised to ride the bus to Chicago, but I'll hike before I'll stay here and do nothing.

Hope you are feeling fine, but should you not be feeling well or have something planned, please tell me and I'll try not to be disappointed. Some of the boys cannot understand why I almost worship you, but you see, they don't know you. Nor do I, but I hope that I can catch more of the gleam that motivates you on and on, over all obstacles for the good of all humanity. You must think the world is very fickle and the general public is a fool, but at the same time one must work for truth's sake and thrust life down their throats, even if they don't have sense enough to appreciate it.

Be thinking about some subjects that would be valuable to research work and tell me those that are essential for good work. Must go now, but think every day of you and thank the Lord for letting me meet you, even for so short a time.

Your friend,
Johnnie Pickle

As WAS HIS HABIT, Professor Carver responded as soon as he got Johnnie's letter. His letter arrived the next week assuring Johnnie that he would be welcome to visit him in Tuskegee. Johnnie knew that he would have to hitchhike but believed that it was a trip he had to take to visit this wonderful, inspiring man of science and God. This might be the last chance he would ever have, he thought.

8-8-32

My beloved boy Mr. Pickle,

Fine, come right on. I will be here except for a few hours only one day this week. While I must go to the Capitol City and meet with the Gov. and the highway man who are interested in the cotton seed building blocks. I will be right back. I am so glad you are coming, "Where there is no vision the people perish." To be sure many people cannot see what you see, never will. There are quite a number of persons who would not be benefited at all by coming. Not so with my dear handsome boy Johnnie. Will save the rest till you come.

Admiringly yours,

G. W. Carver

JOHNNIE WAS IN TUSKEGEE and collected various specimens around the campus with Carver, loving every minute of it. They walked through the fields and woods collecting all sorts of plant and fungal specimens, and as they collected, Dr. Carver would explain what each was, giving the scientific name and life history and life cycles, telling

Johnnie what each was used for. The collecting trip was similar to the one they had in Oxford, Mississippi: eye-opening, educational, and spiritual. Johnnie reveled in the opportunity to learn from this great scientist and scholar. One evening while sitting in Carver's den they started talking about the peanut oil and Carver showed Johnnie what the oil was and how to use it. Johnnie was impressed with the effectiveness of the oil on the area treated on his arm. It felt so good that, when offered, Johnnie took a small bottle for personal use another time.

The days at Tuskegee were over far too soon, but Wisconsin and the challenge of graduate school loomed in the near future. With great honor and humility, Johnnie accepted the offer of Dr. Carver to be one of his Boys. Johnnie bid farewell to his mentor and thanked him for his encouragement and faith in his newest Boy.

Johnnie upon arrival at home immediately wrote Dr. Carver a thank-you note for the experience of learning about nature and the connection between nature and God. Carver's reply was prompt, and he thanked Johnnie for coming to see him and told him that he would be welcome for a repeat visit any time.

8-13-32*

Dear Dr. Carver,

I hardly know what to say to you. This week has been most valuable to me. One is prone to become "degree-minded" and learn nothing. I think it is foolish to make promises, but I think you will find that I shall do all within my power (and with the aid of God) to pass on and build on your work in an altruistic manner. The five dollars, I appreciate and needed. I will never pay that five dollars back to you—unless you need it, but I am going to pass it on. I will have that same chance to help someone else and I will know what it meant to me and what it will mean to the next fellow. The money—pooh! That will soon be gone, but the feeling back of it—that is everything and it kindles my zeal to know that you are so thoughtful midst all of your work and tremendous problems.

Spent Thursday nite [sic] in Birmingham and came home yesterday. Got in about 3:30, tired but happy that I was again able to be with my beloved teacher and friend. A few hardships, yes, but hardships are soon forgotten. I hope that the urge to help to the greatest

---

*   This letter (originally dated 8-13-31) appears to be misdated, as the content suggests this was written by Johnnie after he arrived home from his Tuskegee visit.

of my capacity; that I shall grow and transmit the great work you have started. If I were an excellent writer or an artist, I might be able to thank God, a little for you, but I am not anything but a working boy so I say in the simplest language and in his words, "May the Lord watch between me and thee while we are absent from the other." I might add that—"May the medium of our existence be filled with that insatiable desire to be the greatest service to mankind to the greatest of our ability."

Express my deep gratitude to all those who made it possible for me to have so instructive and delightful a visit, Mrs. Owens especially. Everyone was lovely to me and I learned and enjoyed. To you I will not say thank you, and only grasp your hand and say to God, "Let me see with him."

With deep appreciation and gratitude, I am your friend.

Johnnie Pickle

P.S. Pardon the short letter please, but am packing to go to Wisconsin. Will leave Monday for Oxford—spend Monday nite [sic] and Tuesday there, Wednesday will go to Memphis. Hope to catch bus there to Champaign IL, then from there through Chicago and then to Madison. Will keep you posted to the developments. Love Johnnie.

8-15-32

My beloved boy, Mr. Pickle:

Dear, your card reached me Sun. morning and your fine greeting. It was so good to let me know that you arrived home swiftly.

My dear "Johnnie," just like all of my other precious boys you don't seem to mind very well. I was hoping that you would say nothing about the little enclosure. I wanted my dear handsome boy to have a little extra to get a few comforts if he needed them. I did not mean for you to return it. The joy of having you here is much more than my words can express. You have the spirit, the soul and the vision. I am confident you are going to build upon it. I am now looking forward to the time when you can come again. You only saw a few things this time. You will see many others when you can come back.

I want you to know that to me, you are just my idea of an ideal young man, from every angle. Some day, I believe you will be the head of some research group so that such creative ideas are used for mankind.

I am not at all disturbed by a wandering mind. You have the creative instinct and will develop more of it, when I see you again. I feel that I must have my precious boy long enough to get him started, so that he can go

Left: George Washington Carver posing for a photo as a young man.

Bottom: George Washington Carver with classmates from Iowa State Agricultural College.

George Washington Carver at Lake Geneva in 1892.

Carver painting as a young man.

Nothing brought Carver more joy than his research, and photos of him at work in the laboratory or in the field frequently show him with a smile on his face. He spread that same passion for finding ways to help mankind to his Boys.

Carver's final Boy was Austin Curtis. Curtis was Carver's longtime assistant, but the professor stated that Curtis was more like a son to him. After Carver's death, Curtis helped establish the George Washington Carver Foundation.

Carver received many important guests at Tuskegee, including Franklin Delano Roosevelt (top), Vice President Henry Wallace (bottom), and Henry Ford (facing page).

Carver enjoyed many pastimes, including painting and crocheting. He gifted his creations to those closest to him, just as he gave my father Johnnie a painted card for Christmas.

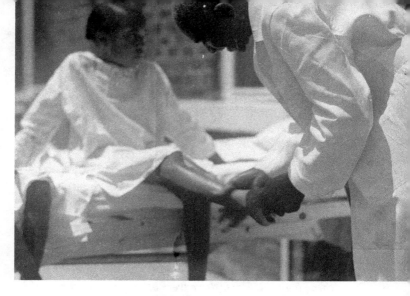

The health of all of God's creatures was important to Carver, who worked on treatments for a variety of illnesses on top of his agricultural efforts. Polio and skin ailments were of particular concern for Carver.

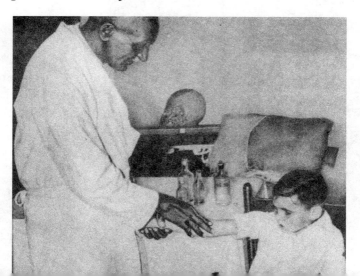

Carver received mountains of mail. While many letters came from his Boys, there were other groups interested in Carver, including doctors and farmers.

Carver was celebrated in his lifetime by those within Tuskegee and without. The university opened the Carver Museum in 1941, established to house his great collections.

on developing. My daily prayers shall follow you. Mrs. Owens and others enjoyed you very much.

With so much love and admiration,

I am sincerely yours.

G. W. Carver

1-31-33

Dear Dr. Carver,

Just a note right now. But in a week or so I hope to know exactly what I think you mean by "Precious Boy."

But I just had to let you know what it is for a bank to bust on one, but really I can truthfully say that it was one of the greatest blessings that ever happened to me: that is, I had to begin working my way surmounting little difficulties and it brought me to you. Hope that you can realize more from your bank than at first seems apparent. And I admire the way you take it, and it strengthens me in my desire to follow your path as best I can.

You might easily have been a statesman. Dr. Carver, to refute without argument and in such a manner as to make the other party feel that he is thinking for himself, is the essence of persuasion. I'll keep my hands off the sparrows. Thanks for two things, a better path and a clean-cut, forceful manner of persuasion. Two well-placed questions tore up more fallacious reasoning than 5 pages of argument could have.

It does my soul good for you to appreciate my letters like that. I hope and pray that my attainments will match the aspirations you have more than helped to plant. It is hard for people here to understand my great love and open admiration of you, but I explain that it is because they don't know you as I do.

I will write again as soon as I have studied and digested Timothy.

A humble disciple,

Johnnie Pickle

EVEN THOUGH JOHNNIE WAS not admitted to the University of Wisconsin in Madison at this time because he had yet to establish residency, he was working toward learning more about himself and life in general. He spent the rest of the year still working at Cleveland's Diner and the YMCA, making some new friends and getting used to the Northern weather. He would write to Dr. Carver several times over the year and of course when he wrote Dr. Carver would respond soon thereafter.

2-2-33

My precious boy, Mr. Pickle:

Your letter is so refreshing. I thought much about you this afternoon. The day was clear and pleasant and I could not resist the call of the wild, and went to the woods for about two hours. I returned with as much as I could carry in my arms. My how I wish I could have had my precious boy "Johnnie" with me, but am truly happy in the thought every day, in the way you are laying the foundation good and deep so that you can carry out the really big things God had in mind for you.

It enthuses me, dear, to know what is possible and how fast you are working towards the goal. Dear, if I had been just a political figure, I never would have had my wonderful little prayer family of dear, dear boys. I would not have been the recipient of this priceless testimonial book, a book of love crystals. If I could get all the money back that I have lost in the two banks, amounting to many thousands of dollars (nearly as many as I am old) for the book, I would without hesitation say no and mean it. Had I been a statesman I would not have known my precious boy "Johnie" [sic]. Your letter dear, is just an expression of what the dear boy is, one of God's chosen vessels. I am truly thankful to God that he has given me the power to love the human race, as you have so beautifully said. If I could not love the God in people, I would truly be miserable and might commit suicide.

With so much love and good wishes for my dear handsome boy.

G. W. Carver

3-17-33

My beloved boy, Mr. Pickle:

Today I have been made very happy as I have before me a letter from two of my precious boys, one attending school at the Univ. of England and the other the Univ. of Wis. Both of these boys are very dear to me. I am so sorry that my dear, handsome boy had to suffer so with his hand, but am happy to learn that it is healing perfectly and without scars of any kind.

Dear the whole country is still in a chaotic state, we do not know what the outcome is going to be. I am just living a day at a time, praying each morning for the strength to last the day through. In all thy ways, dear, acknowledge Him and He shall direct thy paths.

Not a bad thing, to get out on the farm and raise a good living and have some to spare. If you come down, I hope to see you sometime during the summer. Neither of our banks have been able to open, but one may later.

I had such a fine letter from Mr. Lilly (the crippled boy) about two weeks ago. He thinks he can come in the spring. I believe through God, I can help him.

I spoke in Tuscaloosa, Ala. to an audience of more than 1,000: fully 4,000 persons were there but could not get in.

I am not afraid on my dear, handsome boy "Johnie"[sic] disappointing me; as long as God leads, you cannot help but succeed and fit into this new epoch into which we are emerging.

It is so dear for my precious boy to write me; I am always thrilled when I get them.

Yours with genuine love and admiration.

G. W. Carver

THERE IS NO RECORD of what Johnnie did to his hand but apparently he either burned it or injured it. That letter which preceded the above was not found.

In preparing to start school in the fall of 1933, Johnnie sought out a job that would allow him to work and attend classes. Since he had established residence for the fall semester, he needed to find other ways to make a living and provide housing for himself. He found a job with Dr.

E. E. Neff and his wife in the Maple Bluff area of Madison
where many of the wealthier Madisonians had homes. He
was to live above the garage and then serve meals and do
other needed jobs for the doctor and his wife. He left the
job at the diner and the YMCA and decided to go home
to Mississippi for a time in the summer. He also hoped to
return to Tuskegee for a visit with his favorite person in
the world, Dr. George W. Carver.

5-6-33

Dear Dr. Carver,

The closer I came to Mississippi, the stronger my
thoughts turned to you. Got home Wednesday and it
sure is good to be back in Mississippi!

My "Y" job ran out and there wasn't much doing.
By fall I will have already established my residence at
Madison and have an excellent place in Madison to work
and go to school next year. I have a job at a Dr.'s home:
I am expected to be there to wait on the table at noon
and supper, and work there in the afternoon. I have the
mornings and afternoon and evenings free. For this I get,
room and board, $15 a month and have transportation
furnished to and from school. They are very fine people
so I figure that in these times I am very fortunate! It

does seem that God has been looking out for me. I just had to let you know.

I am studying Botany like everything. I have only a key for the North Central and North Eastern plants, but it overlaps quite a bit here. Am getting a text book soon, but haven't yet. The manual that I have is Gray's New Manual of Botany. Right now I'm trying to become acquainted with a little red flower which I believe belongs to the asters. I have seen him twice, but have not had time to talk to him yet.

It may be that I'll get to spend a large part of the summer here. I certainly want to see you before I go north because the next time I go up, it will be for summer and winter for about 3 years. Hope that you are in fine health, and as always Dr. Carver, you are in my thoughts and I would write more but hate to bother you in your splendid work.

Your devoted admirer,
Johnnie Pickle

JOHNNIE SENT A SMALL box with some twigs in it to see if they were infected with some disease and Dr. Carver waited for a while before querying Johnnie as to what he wanted him to do with them.

7-12-33

My beloved boy Mr. Pickle:

Dear, I received a little box from you some days ago, containing three specimens. I have been waiting for a letter from my dear, handsome boy telling me what he wanted me to do with them.

I trust my precious boy is well and happy.

With Love and best wishes.

G. W. Carver

7-20-33

My very own precious boy, Mr. Pickle:

Some how, Dear, I looked for you to come by Tuskegee but am sure your rush to get back did not give my darling boy "Johnie"[sic] time. When you come again I want to keep you much longer, as I want to do some collecting and identifying with you. You are progressing just splendidly and along the lines that are uppermost in my heart. There is no question about your creative mind. You have it and every evidence, as my dear, handsome boy shows of its development, makes me exceedingly happy. As I have said before, you please me from every angle because you are developing and getting acquainted with things.

I am so glad my dear boy like the comments I sent you. By and by I want you to be getting much better ones. Not out of reach at all.

Dear, I get such a delightful thrill when I think that I have as a dear a boy as "Johnie"[sic] one of my dearest and most precious boys who I can watch and see grow into just what God meant when He commanded us to look unto the hills . . .

With genuine love and admiration, I am sincerely yours.

G. W. Carver

IT WAS SEPTEMBER 1933 when Johnnie was awarded residency in the state of Wisconsin and could get serious about his academic quest of a graduate degree in geology. It had been a long year but he had survived. Johnnie sent a letter to Dr. Carver about his new arrangements in Madison and the missed opportunity of the summer.

9-2-33

Dearest Dr. Carver,

My bitterest disappointment of my whole year was that I didn't get to see you. I intended going down, but on July 8, Sat, I got a telegram to be in Madison at 12 o'clock the following Monday. I left everything and here I am. Worked at a restaurant job-salary $15 a week and meals. The first of September I came out to the Dr.'s home that I mentioned last spring. They are very considerate, but I wish you could get hold of them for a while. He and his wife are quite rich and they are quite formal most of the time. I am a general utility man about the place and server for supper (dinner) meals and all day on Sunday. For that I get board, $15 a month and transportation to and from school. I'm expected to be here at noon, the afternoon and at supper, but have mornings and evenings free. I have a room over the garage, a nice room, spacious and beautiful, and also a large bathroom. In there I plan to make my laboratory this year. Tile floor but only hard water. I can make me a table, a reagent shelf, can rent a microscope from the university, Also can buy what things I need and can't use bottles for.

Don't know just exactly how I'm classed at the University, either a graduate student or senior. I hope it's a graduate student—then I'll feel a little freer to do what I want.

Just finished reading the article by Childers in the 1932 October "American", again. He seems to express what I have felt and could not express. Just wanted to tell you that no matter how far it seems that I stray, that down deep there is something that guides me to a life of service—I hope it can half as worthy as yours already has been.

I guess as your work goes you'll kind of forget me, but I can never forget you, because you have become my guiding ideal. Hope I can hang onto the same star that you have, and follow it in the same type of service that you have.

Good nite [sic], Dr. Carver, and always know that here you have a devoted admirer and stumbling follower.

Sincerely,

Johnnie Pickle

9-6-33

My very own precious boy Mr. Pickle:

Your splendid letter has made me so very happy. When I say precious boy . . . Timothy was to him and for the same reason. Paul saw the extension of his work through dear little Timothy, who he loved so dearly that he called him son. I see God's Kingdom extended through the work of my precious boys. I think it so fine that God has thrown such opportunities in your way. He will take care of you. He has promised to do it. You cannot fail. I shall pray for your host and hostess and your fine example will have its influence on them, I am sure.

Dear, how I would love to see your room. I know it is cozy.

When you come to see me next year I hope to have more room in my little den. Some how I feel that you are going to have a wonderful . . . to have . . . return . . . very . . . write . . . the work given me in . . . (July 18,1933)

Forget my precious boy "Johnie", never, not as long as life lasts! You are an inseparable part of my life. I love you as a brother, because God has laid His hand upon you to do creative work for him and make the world better. You are one of my daily comforts. You, dear, help me over many hard places in life. Trials mean nothing when I have such a dear little family.

G. W. Carver

10-14-33

Dearest Dr. Carver,

I'm reading your last letter over. I smiled to myself when I read these lines: "He will take care of you. He has promised to do it." Not at the words but at myself. I fear very soon He'll be put to test. These people I'm staying with are wonderful people but they expect me to donate all this time to their interest. I have about 2.5 hours average to study each day and I need at least five. I'm beginning to hate it here and I shouldn't have room for hate. I'm going to get some other job. I don't know what it will be, but I'm sure it will be better than making a hypocrite out of myself. I'd rather go hungry than do that.

I often think of you in connection with the parable of the sower and thank God that he had prepared me for the seeds you sowed.

I'm now studying Mineralogy, Structural Geology and 4th semester German. I will be able to read both German and French fairly well at the end of the semester. I'll take Descriptive and Analytical Geometry in place of German next semester. Next year I plan to take Organic and Inorganic Chemistry over, and learn it! And also Advanced Botany. I had thought of going ahead and getting a master's degree, but I'd have to take some things I don't care much to have or rather there are things I need and want more.

Every day I feel more certain that God has called me, and I know now wherever and whatever may be my environment that I'll try to dedicate my life toward that goal of Love of Man and in His plan for my life.

I keep a copy of the October "American" on my desk and read it every few days. I always find you a comfort and an inspiration to me.

I'm looking forward to seeing you again, next summer, with a great deal of anticipation. If God is willing, I hope that I may be your disciple and pupil for a little while at least and longer if possible.

Just wanted to say hello, and tell you that each day I realize more clearly that God has given me the power to see things which most men never can see, and that is my call, my duty, my life and I'm glad for the opportunity.

Devotionally yours,

Johnnie Pickle

P.S. Didn't have stamps to mail this and just now able. Sorry, I am quitting the job at Dr. Neff's on the 1st. Will be at the "Y" I guess, don't know what I'll do. My time was being taken up with no chance studying.

JOHNNIE STARTED SCHOOL AT the University of Wisconsin but like most during the Depression struggled to find money to live on. He must have written Dr. Carver about his financial concerns, as Dr. Carver responded with the following letter.

10-21-33

My beloved boy "Johnie":

How very significant your letter has just reached me and in the same mail. Simpson College Bulletin, their college paper from the very college in Iowa where I lived a whole week off of 10 cents.

An editorial is captioned "Simpson Students Use Unique Methods to Stay in College"

(a) Goes into the woods, gathers walnuts, cracks them, gets out the meats and sells them.

(b) Hunts rabbits and sells them.

(c) Peddles eggs.

(d) Sells neck ties. And so on. We had a student here who kept himself in school and assisted his brother by making lye hominy and selling it after school hours. I was teaching then and when we finished the study of corn, I showed them how to make hominy. He had no trouble in selling it as most people like it. I made a little for myself last Thurs. Gave a neighbor a little for his supper, and the entire family ate it and raved over it and are begging me to make more, offer to furnish the corn. It will sell without trouble.

You will make it some way I am perfectly sure. God, I feel confident will lead you in some significant way.

Dear I will be so glad to hear what you work out. A half bushel of corn will make you more than a bushel of hominy. I dare say that with an investment of less than a dollar in cash, you might be able to get a regular group of customers: Hotels, "Cafes" and Restaurants might all take from you. O yes, my boy "Johnie" is going to make inspiring history for himself.

God has given my dear, handsome boy "Johnie" power to see this, you have caught the vision, others will crowd in upon you. I am praying for just this.

With so much love and admiration, with the hope of seeing you next summer without fail.

G. W. Carver

JOHNNIE QUIT HIS JOB at the Neffs and apparently just survived in school. It was difficult catching up on his schoolwork as he was devoting much time to his job at the doctor's. He did survive and finally caught up with his studies, bringing his grades back up to an acceptable level. He seemed to have luck in school and work. It is not known what he was doing for money or if he was back at one of the jobs he had secured before working for the Neffs. He was going to school full time and working full time and just keeping his head above water.

This next letter indicates the recovery that he was going through.

11-8-33

Dear Dr. Carver,

I have been more fortunate than I could have hoped for at first. I have my old meal job back at Cleveland's Lunch with very good hours and am working part time at the "Y" for my room. Right now I am trying to catch up with my studies. The 2 month squander put me behind quite a bit. The courses here are exacting and thorough. I like that.

I'd love to have your recipe for making lye hominy. It sounds good to me and most people here in the city know only the canned hominy. I'll have to cultivate a market but believe it will make a stable market.

I hate to quit any job and believe that this is the only place I have ever left that I could not go back to, if I wanted to. They resent me leaving, but we see life from two completely different points of view—theirs from a capitalistic point of view and I, trying to see from a universal point of view—from the point of view of real democracy for every people on the earth.

I am looking forward to seeing you next summer, and

sometimes I've hoped to see you at Christmas, but I'm afraid that will be in hope. Anyway I read my American every once in a while to keep me in closer touch with you. Tell me what you're doing sometime, and write me whenever you feel that you can spare the time for I am hungry for contact with a personality as fine as yours.

Admiringly and devotionally yours,

Johnnie Pickle

11-10-33

My precious boy, Mr. Pickle:

How happy I am to hear from my dear, handsome boy "Johnie [sic]". "In all thy ways acknowledge Him and He shall direct thy paths". Dear, He seems to be definitely directing your path for which I thank Him so much. I think it splendid.

Under a separate cover I am sending you the recipe for lye hominy. I am having some for my supper here in the "den". Wish you were here to help me enjoy it. Look in Bulletin 39 for the recipe. Dear, I think you will have no trouble in making an attractive product. O yes, make a nice sample, put in a pretty glass jar and sell by the pint or quart at a price low enough to fit the small pocket book. I believe you can work up a fine trade, and you will be surprised at how many nickels and dimes you will take in.

Yes dear, we must get together as soon as convenient. My, wouldn't it be great if you could spend a part of the Christmas holidays with me. I fear your mother would feel badly since you would have such a short time to stay with her. Of course, I would want my dear, handsome boy as long as he could stay.

I just returned from a four days lecture tour in Georgia. I have rarely seen such enthusiasm, and have never had such fine write-ups, some really wonderful editorials.

With so much love, good wishes and admiration for my precious boy "Johnie."

G. W. Carver

2-8-34

Dearest Dr. Carver,

This is Johnnie again, still in school, still searching, hoping, praying and believing that God has called me to give what I can see. Hope He will open my eyes, clear and purify the desire of my heart, always in ideals rest in the type of work you have created, or should say opened to the world.

Sometimes, Dr. Carver, I grow discouraged at my

slowness, fret and chaff at the lost motion, but then again I hope that in spite of my willful wanderings that God will clear my vision.

These people here have an intensity, a methodical manner of treatment, but I miss the depth of soul which drew my heart spontaneously to you. Sometimes, for short periods I lose sight of my visions, almost in a cold sweat I get out alone and I rejoice as I shake off the material shackles that seem to infest this district.

This semester I'm studying Advanced General Botany, Applied Engineering Geology, and Descriptive Geometry. Have a fine group of botany professors—have 4 hours of lab; 2 hours of quiz and 2 hours of lecture each week. We are in the microscopic study of algae at the present time. Every time I look through the microscope a question seems to arise—"How can I make a quantitative analysis of these little filaments?" I like the laboratory much better than the lecture. Lecture is good, but deals now quite a bit with history of plant development in the 6th century to the present time.

Geology course is in the soft-rock mechanics and W. J. Meade is the world authority on it, and I have a fine professor in Descriptive Geometry.

Remember me when you have time and always

know that I think very often of the greatest and finest
man I know.

With deep admiration and love,

Yours,

Johnnie Pickle

2-12-34

My Precious boy "Johnie":

How wonderful to get your precious letter, such a re-
lief from the hectic pile of mail that I am trying to handle.

Since the Associated Press article that went out Dec
30, 1933, with reference to my special peanut oil, (that I
used on you) as a possible aid for infantile paralysis, I have
received to date 1397 letters from suffering humanity.

Not a day passes that I do not think of my dear, handsome boy "Johnie". I have been away more than usual
this fall and winter. I went away with Mr. Hardwick and
a dear sweet boy from Clemson College, SC, on a tour
east. I got back Christmas Eve, was gone a month, have
made two other tours since.

I regret to say that I have not had the time to answer,
or even open but just a few of my Christmas greetings. I
did not get to send out any. Dear you are improving in
every way. I can see it in the way you write. There is much

depth and clearness in the way you express yourself. What a fine foundation you are laying for your creative work.

To be sure, you get tired, with the methodical routine, but by and by, when you become a master of things, you will burst forth with many new creations that will astonish the world. I wish you could know how happy I am over my darling boy "Johnie".

You have been such a comfort to me ever since I met you in Miss. I saw at a glance how richly God had endowed you. Dear in all thy ways acknowledge Him and He will direct thy paths. Keep your hand in His, you cannot fail.

Yes, my precious boy "Johnie" is an ideal boy to me from every angle. How I wish you could go on one of these long trips with Mr. Hardwick and myself. You are doing such fine work, I am happy. May God bless, keep, guide and prosper one of the dearest boys I have ever known.

With so much love, good wishes and admiration, I am sincerely yours.

G. W. Carver

THE FALL SEMESTER AT the University of Wisconsin in 1933 started late for Johnnie but he did catch up. His grades suffered a bit but he remained enrolled. The spring semester went better and finally Johnnie settled into a pattern that allowed him to work, live, and go to school all at the same time. His inspiration came from the knowledge that his Dr. Carver was praying for him and his progress. He, like Dr. Carver, believed that God was directing his path. Knowing my father as I do, I know that he was always reaching out to people and meeting new friends. Somewhere at the University of Wisconsin in these early semesters Johnnie met a group of young men and women with whom he developed friendships, many of which lasted over the years.

4-22-34

Dearest Dr. Carver,

    I have wanted to write several times, but I just hate to take up your time unless I can report definite progress. I'm still in school and am trying to do the best I can. Am taking Descriptive Geometry, Applied Engineering Geometry (really a course of dilating and the behavior of soft rock in open and close packing). We have no text book, and it's really the basics of all of Warren J. Mead's work in Geology, and also Advanced General Botany under Dr. Bryan. Have a fine lab professor too, but is rather young. Don't have much time to study as I have to put in 30 hours a week for room and board and am working 12 more hours besides that. It's pretty hard, but I am still here. A fellow would really like to be able to learn things, but I guess that will come in due course of time. Here's hoping!

How are you? And what are you doing now? Think of you very often and thank God that a man of your caliber came into my life, even for the short time I was with you. It has meant much to me and hope, some day, you won't be disappointed in me.

With deep admiration and love.

Johnnie Pickle

4-24-34

My precious boy "Johnnie":

Your fine letter has just reached me and my how I have enjoyed it. To be sure my dear, handsome boy has been busy. I have as yet not had time to open my Christmas packages. The 1,649 letters from suffering humanity plus the large number of afflicted who come here for consultation and massages keeps me more than busy. It seems fine dear, to be able to help suffering humanity.

I like your course of study so very much, it will fit into the development of your creative mind most admirably. Despite the fact that you are rushed, I know you are getting so much out of it.

I too dear, get very tired at times, along with my other work, I often give 5 massages per day, but thank God I am finding truth. Just what my precious boy "Johnnie", is going to be one of these days. The shoe, my precious boy, should be on the other foot. It is that I am so very, very thankful that I have such a dear boy as you come into my life. It enthuses and encourages me to believe that there is a better day coming for all humanity.

Disappointed in my boy,"Johnnie"? Not by any means. He is just laying a foundation now upon which he will build his mighty structure.

Not a day passes that I do not think of and really thank God for that memorable morning in Miss. where I first saw and met my precious boy, "Johnnie".

With so much love, good wishes and admiration, I am sincerely yours.

G. W. Carver

8-18-34

Dear Dr. Carver,

Had about 10 days home and had planned to come over and surprise you, but my mother's eyes have cataracts on them so I've spent most of my time with her.

Will again be at Wisconsin, and hope that my work

will please you. Always I speak of Dr. Carver and if you get any very curious callers that come from me, just know that I don't mean to take up your time, but do want everyone to know your fine personality and to grasp your vision as much as they can.

May not make school this year, but will be right there digging as best I can.

Was over to Oxford the other day and Mrs. E. N. Lowe gave me a picture of him (Dr. Lowe). I certainly am proud of it. Two of the finest men I have ever known are you and Dr. Lowe. Both of you are eternal to me, and I would love to see you in person now. The only picture I have of you is the one in the October 1932 American, and I cherish it very highly.

Just had to write you while so near, but really you are always near me and I'm very glad that is so.

Love, one of your many admirers,

Johnnie Pickle

8-20-34

My beloved boy "Johnnie":

How I enjoyed your precious letter. I had not heard from my dear, handsome boy in so long that I really looked for you to slip up on me.

Dear, you did the right thing in staying with your angel mother as long as you could. I often sit and think how happy you have made me. How inspiring it is to meet those great souls upon whom God has laid his hand to do special work. Never a day passes that we do not meet in spirit.

Dear, the food section of the U.S. Dept. of Agriculture has worked out a commercial method of making chips from sweet potatoes that they claim is superior to the white potato chip. This may open a possibility for helping many a poor boy through school, just as lye hominy has.

I am hoping your mother's eyes will be better soon; impaired vision is so annoying. How fine, dear that you could get a picture of Dr. Lowe, one of God's noblemen. Son, I do not believe that I belong in that class. I wish I did. My dear boy "Johnnie" does however.

I wish that you could see the pile of 1,873 letters piled high on my desk, all from suffering humanity, then scores and scores of people come to see me. My entire day on Sundays, are given to the afflicted. I do not pretend to go to church. I am trying to work out a great truth for humanity. Dear, the little bottle of clear peanut oil you saw and had used on you, started the investigation.

I do so firmly believe my precious boy "Johnnie" will
do something, some day, just as pronounced.

With so much love and admiration,

G. W. Carver

JOHNNIE WAS STILL WORKING toward his geology degree
in the fall of 1935 but was apparently considering changing his focus to education. His grades were fine but the
satisfaction and drive required seemed to be changing. So,
without completing his master's degree in geology, even
though he had enough hours, Johnnie changed his major to
education in the spring semester of 1936. He had to swal-
low his pride and make the switch. No paper trail of com-
munications to Dr. Carver indicates that he had changed,
only the transcript from the University of Wisconsin. The
records department at the university was questioned and
they could not explain why he did not have two master's
degrees. Since Dr. Carver was a masterful teacher he would
not have been disappointed in the change but would have
encouraged Johnnie to keep on progressing.

Johnnie wrote to Dr. Carver less and less in an attempt
to not take time from the valuable work Carver was doing
with his peanut-oil massages. Despite an Associated Press
article in 1933 indicating that Carver had found a cure

for polio, the professor never claimed that to be so and no amount of denying that statement would stop the flood of letters and people attempting to get to Tuskegee for a treatment. Once the article was published, suffering people all over the world beat a path to Tuskegee to beg for treatment and curing. The suffering people would not listen to Carver's disclaimers of a miracle cure. George Carver was in demand and he would attempt to help those he could and reject those that he thought either lacked faith in healing or did not meet certain medical criteria. The medical community as a whole rejected the potential for peanut oil plus massage in curing polio and many fought hard against anyone making a curative claim. No one ever proved that it did not work and eventually Dr. Carver had some two-hundred-plus patients who attributed their improvement to the peanut oil. The medical community never did accept the peanut-oil-massage treatment as an effective option.

In the late fall of 1934 Johnnie apparently had a double hernia and wrote his mentor about his medical problem. He underwent surgery, healed rapidly, and was back in school as soon as he could get on his feet.

12-23-34

My beloved boy Mr. Pickle:

Before your letter reached me, according to your schedule the operation had been performed. I do hope my dear handsome boy will be out soon, and that you will be renewed in strength and vigor. Dear, since it had to be done, now is an excellent time. I am glad you told me as I at once put you, especially, on my prayer budget, that the Great Physician will visit you with His healing power.

No, my dear boy, I am not by any means fine, but have one of the finest boys I know in the person of Johnny [sic] Pickle.

Let me hear from you right away please, get the nurse to write if they want you to be quiet. Your improvement and rapid recovery will make me exceedingly happy. To be sure I shall not tell your parents, your dear mother would worry herself sick.

With so much love and admiration for my dear boy, I am sincerely yours.

G. W. Carver

THERE IS ANOTHER MISSING letter from Johnnie indicating that his healing was going well and that he was back on his feet and working. He was still in geology studies for both the fall and spring semesters. He was working long hours and going to school.

12-31-34

My precious boy Johnie:

My but your letter is refreshing. Just to know that the operations are over and that you will soon be a well man. It was very dear of you to let me know. I did not worry much as I felt all the time that God would bless the means to the healing thereof.

Well dear, I have to stop, give two massages and get a visitor located at Dorothy Hall, where you stayed.

My work is on infantile paralysis, underweights, acne and nervous people. God is blessing these peanut oils in such a wonderful way. Dear, do not write until you can sit up as I shall not worry at all now.

May God ever bless and keep my dear boy.

G. W. Carver

THERE IS ANOTHER MISSING letter from Johnnie to Dr. Carver as the response indicates communication about Johnnie's recovery progress.

1-8-35

My precious boy "Johnie [sic]":

It was so dear of you to write and let me know how you were progressing. It is impossible for you to know how happy I am that both operations are over and that you are out. The Great Physician can do wonders when He comes with healing power.

We are having right now a miniature electric storm. The rain is heavy. I am so glad dear, that you have met Mr. Collins: He is a prince of a fellow. Should it come in handy, please remember me to him.

I do feel so happy over my precious boy "Johnie", for whom I thank God, O so often for permitting our paths to meet.

With love and genuine admiration,

G. W. Carver

P.S. Son, be very careful and do not strain yourself much until thoroughly healed and strong

THE SPRING SEMESTER WAS over and nothing much had changed for Johnnie. He was still working at the diner and the YMCA but apparently changed living arrangements now to the University Club and was still taking large doses of geology.

10-20-35

Dearest Dr. Carver,

Have been thinking of you so much of late that I decided I'd write. I'm still in the University of Wisconsin. I'm taking Petrology under Dr. Winchell, Quantitative Analysis and Economic Geology. I'm hoping to take Master's degree and prelims in June. There are many things I want but realize that I must also live while studying, therefore I'm hoping to get enough Geology to teach until I can support myself in our Synthetic Aspirations.

Often think of you and always I count you as one of the greatest blessings of my life. Take care of yourself and write me when you can.

With admiration and respect, I am sincerely yours.

Johnnie Pickle

10-23-35

My dear boy Johnny [sic]:

How delighted I am to get your splendid letter, which just reached me. I had not heard from you for so long that I was wondering just what had happened. I am glad it was nothing serious.

It is fine that you are back in school, and making splendid progress. Your subjects seem unusually interesting, and will fit into what you want most admirably. It is needless of me to say to you that not a day passes that I do not think of my boy Johnny. How thankful I am to the Giver of All Good Gifts that he made you come into my life.

My work has grown even more strenuous than in previous years, as that of infantile paralysis is absorbing all of my time. I am getting such excellent results, so much so, physicians are beginning to give it real serious consideration. I have a number of cases that physicians said could not be helped, which are responding to the peanut oil treatment most admirably.

With much love and best wishes, I am Very sincerely yours.

G. W. Carver, Director
Research and Experiment Station
GWD-enh

NOW DR. CARVER HAD a secretarial assistant indicating that the demands upon his time and energy were taking a toll, as he continued to work hard even though he was aging.

Johnnie traveled back home to Aberdeen after the spring semester and fell in love with Scottie Brown. She followed him back to Madison, took classes, and entered a beauty contest run by Sigma Xi fraternity. She was voted a top-ten beauty. Scottie and Johnnie were a good match in that they were both brought up in the local scouting programs and active in both swimming and other outdoor skills. They were engaged and married in September 1936. Surprisingly Johnnie did not inform Dr. Carver that he had met his romantic match, changed his major, and completed his master's degree. Scottie and Johnnie had their first child in late June of 1937. Johnnie finally wrote Dr. Carver announcing both his marriage and the birth of his first child: a daughter, Patricia. There is no copy of the letter Johnnie wrote but a response from Dr. Carver, as usual, was received soon after delivery of Johnnie's letter.

1-13-38

My beloved friend Mr. Pickle:

How delighted I am to get your fine letter, and especially from little Patricia, which is enthusiastically surprising and pleasing. I am especially happy to get greetings from the young lady. She looks every inch of fine greetings, and looks like she really means it. What a joy she must be to you and Mrs. Pickle. I am sure you are exceedingly happy. I am pleased that you are getting along so nicely, and all is going well with you.

I regret that my strength is not as good as it was when
I saw you, but I am thankful that I am able to be up.

If you have not read the article in the January 8th
issue of Liberty, I am sure that you will be interested in it.

Wishing you and yours the finest things that can
possible come to you, I am

Yours very truly,

G. W. Carver, Director

Agriculture Research and Experiment Station

Enh

DR. CARVER FELL DOWN the stairs in Dorothy Hall in
1938. This fall resulted in significant debilitation on his
part. Due to the fall along with a continued problem with
pernicious anemia, his health continued to deteriorate
until his death in 1943. Carver's activity became less
and less with Dr. Austin Curtis, his assistant and friend,
providing support and protection. There are no more letters exchanged between Johnnie Pickle and the famous
scientist. Henry Ford had the elevator put in especially
for Carver and Austin Curtis was accompanying Carver
pretty much everywhere, attempting to protect him from
stressful situations and physical overreach.

Carver still had significant influence on Johnnie's life

and work. Johnnie, his wife Scottie, and their daughter Patricia moved to Columbus, Mississippi. Jobs were still tight, even for college graduates. Johnnie and Scottie's second child John Jr. (the author of this book) was born in 1939. Finally Johnnie landed a job with DuPont in Memphis, Tennessee, in the manufacture of explosives at their plant there. Their third child Stewart was born in Memphis in 1942. DuPont transferred Johnnie to their plant in Pryor, Oklahoma, where they stayed until the war started slowing down. Their fourth child Ken was born in Pryor in 1944. DuPont closed the plant and Johnnie was blessed in that he found a position at a small Christian university, John Brown University, in Siloam Springs, Arkansas. The final four children (David born in 1947, Katherine born in 1952, Sharon born in 1955, and Jim born in 1958) were all born in the local hospital in Siloam Springs. Johnnie served in a number of capacities on the university staff, including teaching positions in the education department. Johnnie finally did achieve his Ed.D. from the University of Arkansas in 1951. These accomplishments would have pleased his mentor George W. Carver.

One of the ways that Carver influenced the Pickle family lays in the achievements and careers of Johnnie and Scottie's children. There are two doctorate degrees, three

The Pickle family in 1957. Back row, left to right:
Stewart, Pat, John Jr., and Kenneth. Front row,
left to right: David, Kathy, Johnnie, Jimmy,
Katherine Scott, and Sharon.

master's, two bachelor's, and one skilled heavy- equipment
operator and truck driver. Two of the children, Pat and
Stewart, and their spouses served God as missionaries to
carry the gospel to other lands and peoples.* Pat taught

---

*   Pat and her husband served in Taiwan. Stewart and his wife served
     in Ecuador and then in the United States, including Florida, Texas,
     and Alaska, starting new Spanish-speaking churches.

young people for the rest of her award-winning career in the US and Europe. Three of the sons served in the military: John Jr., Ken, and Jim, the latter two spending their careers serving their country, retiring as high-ranking command officers. John Jr. completed his graduate degrees and served Oklahoma State University as an agricultural extension entomologist in the southwest Oklahoma area for two years. He then spent the next twenty-nine years working for industry in product development. The two younger daughters both earned college degrees, one as an artist and the other in recreational leadership, making their own marks in their churches and communities. David, the middle son, took courses in engineering, construction, and ecology but never finished a college degree. David also wrote the first paper in the family on G. W. Carver and the fourth kingdom, the synthetic kingdom. David and his wife (Donna) are the owners of the family property, which was proudly known as Kamp Paddle Trails, a summer camp for forty years sharing nature and outdoor skills with young people from all over the United States and some foreign countries.

Each of the Pickle children served their community, state, and nation and spent decades teaching all sorts of skills to young people at the camp and others through

The Pickle family in 2011. Standing, left to right:
John Jr., Kathy, Jim, Kenneth, Sharon, David,
and Stewart. Seated: Pat.

their churches, schools, and social and professional groups. Carver would approve of the efforts that he instigated through his "Boy" Johnnie Pickle. Each of the Pickle children reached out to all peoples in their endeavors and magnified the "Carver effect" as demonstrated by this magnificent soul named George W. Carver. Then each of the Pickle children passed it forward to their children (eighteen in total), each in their own diverse fields from art to academics to law enforcement and business. Now the next generation is in progress and the "Carver effect" continues to grow and be passed forward.

The impact on the lives of those young people who attended the summer camps at Kamp Paddle Trails (KPT) near Watts, Oklahoma, is an impact that is still being felt. Each summer since the camp ceased operations in 1991, there have been adults who attended or worked at KPT who contact the owners or one of the other Pickle children to come back to KPT to have a sort of reunion. The summer visits involve walking the hiking trails up to the bluffs, swimming in the beautiful Illinois River, fishing, canoeing, and sitting around a campfire singing old camp songs, which usually brings tears of joy in remembering those wonderful camp and personal experiences. Over the forty years that KPT was active, hundreds of children were impacted by learning things they couldn't get at home and having fun in a healthy and wholesome environment, surrounded by Carver's Great Creator's world. There must have been approximately eight thousand campers to attend, experiencing nature and learning outdoor skills deep in God's wonderful creation, loving and remembering it their entire lives. Now they return, bringing children, grandchildren, and friends so they too can see where the old campers spent some of the most wonderful days of their lives.

Johnnie's impact on college students was also passed on through his teaching and personal interaction skills. For many years after Johnnie's death in 1981, students, upon returning to homecoming reunions at John Brown University, would contact the family to tell them how much they learned from and appreciated Dr. John H. Pickle of JBU.

4

Why This Man?

Why would George W. Carver believe that he would be a good mentor for young men trying to make their mark in life? Well, he was a natural teacher and an excellent communicator; had natural empathy for young people and always challenged them to use their own brains; and was very practical and, according to Booker T. Washington, a great common-sense problem solver. These skills and talents enabled George W. Carver to become the expert who could answer almost any question that his students or Boys might have. Carver utilized the skill of Socratic questioning like an art form to get the person asking a question to answer it themselves. Carver's students and especially his Boys were considered his children and he treated them so. The students returned the favor and treated him like their father and the relationship was very rewarding. A couple of his students excelled sufficiently to be sought out by the USDA to be agricultural extension agents, the first of their race in the nation. This must have started Carver thinking about how he could work on the race-relations problems faced in the South. He decided that he would find young men who might be able to help him address this race issue and still meet Carver's goal of educating young people.

At that time in his life Carver was a gifted motivational speaker and was in high demand all over the South. As he went from school to school and speech to speech, he found young people that were raised in a Christian environment who seemed to want to grow in their academic ability and at the same time help bridge the race issues of the time. Usually at the end of a speech those young people who were inspired and excited about Carver would rush to the stage and want to talk more and shake his hand. Carver would meet most of "His Boys" in these situations and if the occasion presented itself, Carver would invite the person to join his little family of Boys. No one knows exactly how many were invited and accepted the invitation but the number is thought to be more than fifty young people. This special group of young men was by invitation only. You did not join it as a credit; you were invited by the Wizard of Tuskegee himself to become part of his prayer family because he felt an unspoken connection. Most were white but there were some of color. This author has not found any women in that group but suspects that being female was not a contrived limitation but rather can be chalked up simply to never having the chance to meet them in this public-speaking environment. Carver prayed with and for his Boys, exchanged letters with them, and answered any questions they might have from course work, job changes, life experiences, or love. There was no limitation. Carver as a mentor and person was very familiar with these young people and they him. The experience each of these young people had was expressed as a life-changing and life-lasting event. Carver loved them like his own sons and in return the Boys went on with their lives, some continuing education, some getting jobs and asking for advice, some asking questions about religion, prayer, love, and marriage. Carver started this activity in 1922 and continued until 1935 when he finally got a young man named Austin W. Curtis, Ph.D., to be his last and final Boy and true research assistant. Curtis once stated that "he was trained by Cornell University and educated by George W. Carver."

I ask myself, "Why would those who became his Boys accept the role of being mentored by George W. Carver?" These young men were already college graduates or would be soon and starting out in their careers. They were Christians and had family who would also help them. What follows is a list of attributes that explains why Carver was a great mentor.

Carver was:

1. Famous in that he had already done much of his research on peanuts, sweet potato, pecans, and cotton. He was always looking to increase that knowledge through research in God's little workshop.

2. Extremely well educated in agriculture, including plants, animals, crop sciences, chemistry, and mycology. He was very alert in nature and understood the ecology of the environment.

3. An outstanding motivational teacher of both young college students and adults. Crowds of four thousand to five thousand people were not uncommon.

4. A very dedicated Christian and Bible scholar. He was a strong believer that prayer answered problems. He encouraged his charges to read the Bible and to seek advice from the same.

5. A very demanding and disciplined instructor but very fair and student supporting. He had great empathy for those who wanted to learn and little patience for those who did not.

6. A diverse, talented artist in music, painting, needle work, carving, poetry, and other forms of art.

7. A chef-quality cook of both home cooking and creative dishes that he made from scratch.

8. A talented and creative problem solver of most any issue. He would always solve a problem based on need and cost where possible. He made most of the laboratory equipment to do his early research from items that he and his students salvaged from the local dump, cast off items from the public in Tuskegee, and back alleys in town.

9. Well traveled in the United States and had experienced much in the process.

10. Tireless in his efforts to create racial tolerance and acceptance between Black and white people.

11. A survivor of Jim Crow Laws and significant racial prejudice in life.

12. An experienced user of the Socratic teaching method that encourages students to answer their own questions.

13. A cultivator of strong personal relationships with his students and "his Boys" that lasted a lifetime.

14. Friends with powerful and important figures that he regularly communicated with.

15. Lifelong friends with Black and white communities, male and female.

16. A wise and trusted friend to both students and "his Boys."

17. A proponent of pushing those he mentored to reach for more than they thought they could accomplish and use their own brain to achieve their goals.

18. Inspired to have his students be who they could be and pass it on to others.

19. Motivated to have his students and Boys be morally strong, honest, clean both inside and out, and helpers in creating racial acceptance and justice.

20. Writer of forty-four bulletins directed at and for the poor Black farmer in the South in an effort to push, drag, or pull them out of their downtrodden state of living by using a scientific approach to farming.

Putting aside why Carver was so beloved by his Boys, there's no question that Carver meant everything to them. A "Remembrance Book" was given to Carver in 1932, including letters from each of the known forty-seven Boys. Writing to Johnnie Pickle, Carver called the book the most crystallized demonstration of love he had ever seen. He was moved over the book and cherished it. Tragically, this book was destroyed in a fire that damaged much of the

George W. Carver Museum in Tuskegee in 1947.

The influence of the life of this great man is something like a large stone being tossed into the glass-slick surface of a pond. Upon breaking the water, the rock causes radiating waves to make their way to the shore and back again. Each wave seeks out obstacles surrounding it and moves on, then back again, until all of the energy is utilized. Such was Carver's effect on his Boys, who radiated out from him and brought significant change to their own personal world.

Resources

Especially recommended.

Allhoff, Fred. "Black Man's Miracles: The Story of a Great and Good American." *Liberty Magazine.* January 1938.

Burchard, Peter Duncan. *Carver: A Great Soul.* Fairfax: Serpent Wise, 1998.

*Burchard, Peter Duncan. *George Washington Carver: For His Time and Ours.* Diamond: George Washington Carver National Monument, 2005. Burchard's well-referenced manuscript was funded by the George Washington Carver National Monument.

Borth, Christy. *Pioneers of Plenty: The Story of Chemurgy.* New York: Bobbs-Merrill Company, 1939.

Brown, Clarence Richard. *The Pickle and Brown Historical Records and Photographs.* Unpublished, 2010.

Childers, James Saxon. "A Boy who was Traded for a Horse." *American Magazine.* October 1932.

Clark, Glenn. *The Man Who Talks with the Flowers.* St. Paul: Macalester Park Publishing, 1939.

*Edwards, Ethyl. *Carver of Tuskegee.* Self-published, 1976. Edwards consulted with Jim Hardwick, who Carver considered his number one spiritual Boy. Hardwick provided Edwards personal and historical information based on some three hundred letters he exchanged with Carver.

*Elliott, Lawrence. *George Washington Carver: The Man Who Overcame.* Englewood Cliffs: Prentice-Hall Inc., 1966. Elliott visited and interviewed a number of Carver's friends and fellow staff members at Tuskegee Institute.

Hersey, Mark D. *My Work Is That of Conservation: An Environmental Biography of George Washington Carver.* Athens: University of Georgia Press, 2011.

Gart, Jason H. *He Shall Direct Thy Paths: The Early Life of George W. Carver.* National Park Service, 2014.

*Holt, Rackham. *George Washington Carver: An American Biography.* Garden City: Doubleday, Doran and Company Inc., 1943. Holt visited Carver on the campus of Tuskegee Institute. She was assisted in writing the biography by Dr. Austin Curtis Jr., Carver's research associate from 1935 to his death.

*Kremer, Gary R. *George Washington Carver: In His Own Words.* Columbia: University of Missouri Press, 1987.

CPSIA information can be obtained
at www.ICGtesting.com
Printed in the USA
LVHW082358260722
724506LV00015B/66